THE

Gift

OF A

Listening

Heart

A Path to Healing

Elizabeth Reis

OTHER BOOKS BY ELIZABETH REIS, SSJ:

A DEEPER KIND OF TRUTH

A TRAINING MANUAL FOR FACILITATORS

THE GIFT OF A LISTENING HEART

A Path to Healing

by
Elizabeth Reis, SSJ

PUBLISHED BY:
Center Space Publishing
32260 - 88th Avenue
Lawton, MI 49065

ISBN: 978-0-9857480-8-1

Cover and Book Design by Penny Kelly

TABLE OF CONTENTS

ACKNOWLEDGMENTS

So many people played a role in bringing my ideas and understanding to the point that this book emerged that it is difficult to thank them all. However, special recognition simply must go to:

Michael J. Howell
and
Jennybelle P. Rardin

...for each believed in me, encouraged and supported me, and continue to teach me how to be faithful to myself, to them, and to the God who brought us together.

Acknowledgment must also go to:

...the Human Resource Staff at General Motors in Kalamazoo, MI who have been a continual source of strength, humor, and optimism!

...UAW representatives Larry Martin, Jim Cool, along with General Motor's staff representatives, Jim Frenthaway, and Jannie Williams.

...to my Students and Facilitators Gloria Copeland, Carolyn Daily, Mary Runchey, Michelle Reineck, Penny Robinson, Mary Therese Meagher, Dolores Livernois, Jill Waskowski, Amy Pifer, Barbara Gourley, and countless students of *The Art of Listening* classes.

...and to Penny Kelly, an awesome editor, scholar, and friend, in gratitude for a lifetime of service as editor, printer, and publisher of deeply holy manuscripts that continue to benefit an ageless world.

DEDICATION

This book is dedicated to
all those who have
suffered through years of
misunderstanding,
misjudgment
and the feeling that,
"Nobody listens to me!"
May they discover
that part of the problem
is that few people
know *how* to listen any more.
If each of us could learn
how to really listen,
it would teach others...
and slowly but surely
the world would become
a wonderful place.

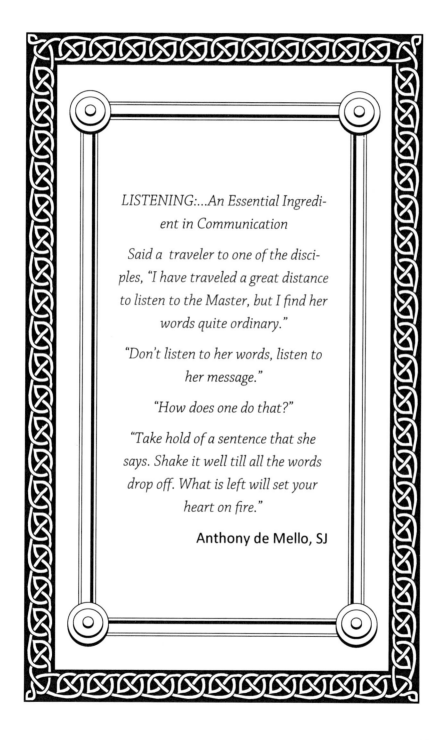

LISTENING:...An Essential Ingredient in Communication

Said a traveler to one of the disciples, "I have traveled a great distance to listen to the Master, but I find her words quite ordinary."

"Don't listen to her words, listen to her message."

"How does one do that?"

"Take hold of a sentence that she says. Shake it well till all the words drop off. What is left will set your heart on fire."

Anthony de Mello, SJ

9

Preface

❧❧

The Gift of a Listening Heart

Course manual for...
The Art of Listening Seminar

The Gift of a Listening Heart is the book that accompanies the *Art of Listening* seminar. Both book and seminar seek to present **listening** as a communication skill. The book has been written as a course manual to be used for the training of ordinary, everyday people who can work as facilitators for deep listening.

Within its pages you will find the basic philosophy of the course along with stories, application methods, reflection of experiences, and other insights that I have collected and taught for many years.

I first learned the style of listening presented in this book in 1971 under the remarkable direction of Charles A. Curran, PhD, a psychology professor at Loyola University and founder of the Counseling-Learning Institute in Chicago. Curran himself based many of his insights on the non-directive method developed by Carl Rogers, under whom he studied.

When I first began to design the content for teaching this seminar to the general pubic, I presumed that the participants who came wanted to learn connective communication. However, it soon became clear that there were a few who were there to teach the staff how to do it! That was an interesting wake-up call!!

I soon began to recognize the variety of speakers there are in the world. We then added another set of presentations about different kinds of speakers for whom this kind of connection was not the purpose for some of their conversation. We also added some 'qualities' to the role of speaker.

∂∾✑

The method used in the seminar is one in which the presenter is introduced as the SPEAKER/KNOWER. The participants are asked to step into the role of LISTENER/LEARNER. Descriptions of the expectations for both the KNOWER and the LEARNER are carefully explained by the presenter. Two or three experienced facilitators will also be present among the listeners.

Then, presentations are given to the group for about 1½ hours. During the time of each group presentation, the students listen and watch the interactions between presenter and facilitators, who are verbally reflecting what they hear at both the *cognitive* (thinking) and *affective* (feeling) levels. The facilitators help demonstrate the process, and this helps the students to grasp what focused listening is.

The participants are then invited to give reflective responses as soon as they understand the process as it is being modeled by the facilitators. There is a short break after the group presentation, and

꙳

then the large group is divided into smaller groups of 4-6 people and asked to share the material taught in the presentation using the same method of listening as demonstrated by the facilitators.

Each person in the group is given 10 minutes. For the first 5 minutes of that period, one of the group will be the speaker/knower, and one other person in the group will be the listener/learner. The rest of the group will act as silent observers and listeners.

When the first 5 minutes are up, the remaining 5 minutes are used for an evaluation of the experience by both the speaker and the listener. Each shares their observations of the experience of being listened to without interruption, or of the challenges of having to listen without interjecting their own ideas. During this time, the facilitators spend some time at each table to help them learn the techniques, clarify any confusions, and support the learning process. When each person in the small group has experienced being both listener and speaker, the participants return to the large group for a session called: Surprises and Discoveries. This section of the seminar gives everyone a chance to share how it felt to be heard, and to again clarify any part of the process that might not yet be understood.

The content of the seminar can usually be covered in about 24 hours, usually in three 8-hour days. During that time, both the presenter and the facilitators are available to the participants for any questions or insights that might be helpful.

This seminar has been offered to a variety of groups: educators, business people, church ministers, hospital professionals, or married and single adults who want to improve their skills within relationships, families, or work settings.

With well over 20 years of experience in presenting this seminar, the staff of the Counseling-Learning Institute has found that this style of listening is not only professionally effective but is also a remarkable tool for personal transformation.

This book has been written as a personal response to the facilitators who have so generously and skillfully helped in the presentation of this material, and who have patiently asked us for a book that supports the further development of the art of listening.

Elizabeth M. Reis, SSJ
February 14, 2017

INTRODUCTION
༃ঌ

Consistent surveys taken today in relationships, education, and business reveal the desperate need for what is commonly called *communication*. As a result of such surveys, uncounted thousands are put through communication workshops, programs, experiences, or counseling situations as a response to this need. Participants walk away with degrees, diplomas and/or certificates assuring both the participant and the world that 'communication' is now a proven skill. The person returns to the world of people and machines and often, in spite of the magic piece of paper, there is still something missing...and another survey or course is taken.

Did the participants fail? Or was there, rather, a missing ingredient in the uncounted seminars on communication? Whenever we read or study another well-planned program written in response to this obvious communication need in our society, there is one ingredient either missing or only superficially considered: **listening**.

The ability, desire, and/or awareness of the need for listeners is far more serious than we can imagine!

Often the courses in communication allow a person to discover his/her need to talk. They present excellent skills for public speaking, personal debate, and/or confidence in sharing insights and feelings. But do they create caring, sensitive, active listeners? We encourage group dynamics in which the participants 'perform' before an audience but seldom invite careful, safe, one-on-one opportunities to touch the raw parts of ourselves with an understanding, listening, accepting, and non-judgmental partner.

This book addresses that missing link. We will initially consider the wider world of communication with its many facets and possibilities: debates, questioning, skilled presentation by 'a knower' with equal responses from 'learners.'

The wider world of communication accepts questions, directions, advice, dialogue, debate, and/or conflict. This intellectual style of communication is well-practiced and rewarded in our hierarchical society. Therefore, we have too many 'knowers' and too few 'learners.'

Even in our commitment to relational connections and conversations we have many people who need to be the 'speaker' (knower) and very few willing to be a 'listener' (learner). Often in the midst of a speaker's conversation, the listener interrupts with their own personal experiences and information. A non-judgmental, receptive learning stance is what is often missing in our verbal exchange.

When was the last time someone gave you their undivided attention? Who was the last person that listened to you without judgment or advice? When did you last carefully and compassionately hear another without expressing your own opinion? This is not an examination of conscience for one's sins! Few of us are deliberately thoughtless. We are only unaware, unskilled, and inattentive people who want desperately to be heard and understood (and agreed with perhaps) but are not able to hear another person with an open and understanding heart.

In order to learn to hear beyond the words and hear the heart, a listener must let go of the need to speak or convince. This is true whether one wants to hear the heart of another, wants to hear their own deepest heart, or wants to hear the heart of God. When Jesus invited us to 'die to ourselves so another may live,' he might well have been talking about the kind of 'dying' it takes to *totally* listen, putting aside all our own personal insights, experience, and information in order to understand another without an agenda.

Wise King Solomon knew about this kind of listening. We find him pleading for it in 1 Kings 3:5, 7:9-13 when God offered Solomon whatever he wanted.

In Gibeon, Solomon had a vision of the Lord in a dream by night; and God said to him, "Ask for whatever you want and I will give it to you."

Solomon answered saying, "O Lord, my God, you have made your servant king in the place of David my father, and I am only a young boy with no knowledge of how to go out or come in. Give your servant then a discerning (and listening) heart to govern your people and to distinguish between right and wrong. For who is able to be the judge of this great people?"

The Lord was pleased that Solomon had asked for this. So God said to him, "Because your request is for a wise heart and not for long life for yourself or for wealth or for the destruction of your enemies, but for discernment, I will do as you have asked. I will give you a heart so wise and understanding that there has never been your equal in the past and never will there be any like you in the future. Moreover, I will give you what you have not asked for: both riches and honor, so that in your lifetime you will have no equal among kings."

This book is designed to be a course in itself. It will help you recall what you will hear in the practice sessions and will help to guide you in your day-to-day communications. However, reading this book will not do the whole job for you. Modeling, directing, practicing, and polishing are not something one learns by reading; they are learned by seeing, hearing, and doing.

Just as in the live seminars on *The Art of Listening*, there are pages in this book titled *Thoughts, Notes, and Ideas*. These are workbook pages on which you can record your thoughts, impressions, ideas, *Aha!* moments, and other important things you discover as you learn how to listen and communicate well. When you look back long after the course is finished, the *Thoughts, Notes, and Ideas* pages will help you remember and enjoy what you have learned.

It is hoped that this book will be a trigger mechanism that will help you begin to practice and polish your ability to give the gift of a listening heart. Each chapter will help you recall and go deeper with the principles presented in the course. In the live seminar, the instructor and the facilitators will model the skills, and as a listening trainee you are encouraged to go deeper and practice daily in order to become a skilled listener yourself, and to model this art to everyone around you.

Chapters 1, 2, 3, and 4 teach you how to step into the role of *listener* and be more cooperative and less abrasive in your communications. You will be introduced to the roles and stages of development of *Speaker/Listener*, and *Knower/Learner*. As you step into these roles you will also be asked to assume certain qualities needed for the role.

Chapters 5, 6, 7, and 8 teach you how to apply the techniques and attitudes learned in a variety of situations and to develop and fine-tune your listening skills in non-verbal communication. We will also look at those cultural factors that you should be aware of in your own life so that you are not blocked by them in your efforts to be a *listener*.

This is truly a 'course-in-a-book!' At the end of the book, we will take the time to examine the various ways that people communicate with one another, but in the beginning, we will focus only on listening.

If you are taking this course in a live workshop, during the group presentations, you will be presented with the obstacles and dynamics involved in listening: fear, emotional blocks, belief systems, your historical and cultural inheritance, and the responses each of us might make because of all these ingredients mixed together in each of us. We will consider each of these dynamics in relation to *listening*. As you begin to see the relationships that exist between the skill and the *listening*, you will hopefully be better able to choose the kind of responses you want to make in any setting.

Whether you are attending a live workshop or working through the book on your own, you must hold yourself to the role of *listening*. If, during the presentations, you begin to use any of the other communication skills, you will trip yourself up and must go back again to the primary purpose for which you came – to learn *listening*, which is the essential ingredient not only in communication but also in human belonging.

Chapter 1

❧❦

THE NEED FOR LISTENERS

HE LEFT THE BOSS' OFFICE DISCOURAGED AND AFRAID. THE information given him had held an accusing note. He didn't dare say so…his job was in jeopardy. The few minutes with the boss had left him confused and angry. Within minutes he met a co-worker who asked, "How are you doing?" Was this a flippant remark or an invitation to share his struggle? He if answered truthfully, what response would he receive from the questioner? Did he dare hope for a listening heart? Again…fear, mistrust.

She smiled, and drank her coffee among the three friends who frequently met after work. The smile hid the pain of knowing her husband was having an affair with another woman. Everyone else had such happy marriages! With whom could she dare share it? She had tried once and the flippant answer had been, "Hang in there, it will get better. You know how men are." Advice, disinterest, rose-colored words of assurance… these were all she seemed to receive when her heart needed to be heard and understood.

The young artist was waiting at the restaurant for his friend to arrive. He could hardly wait to tell his friend that his first painting had sold, and at $2000! Would his friend hear and rejoice with him in his excitement, amazement, almost awe at such an accomplishment? Would he understand? How could he share it without sounding like he was bragging?

These three stories are examples of the universal struggle going on in communication today. The missing ingredient in each situation is *listening!* The main character in each situation is either not experiencing or not expecting to be listened to. There are no villains, just human beings who haven't yet learned the skills of hearing beyond the words.

We have been taught well how to give advice, directions, perhaps even inspiration. We have NOT been taught to listen. Is true listening possible? Is it feasible in our busy world of computers and deadlines? Perhaps a more important question is: Do we dare to continue life and career without these essential listening skills?

Past Attitudes

Most people have been taught that life will be happy and successful if we know either 'the right information' or 'the right people.' Our culture and time have been dedicated to education and leadership. These are noble pursuits. Yet once acquired, how will they be used?

Success in the past often depended on how much power you could wield. Authority was frequently exercised without question. To listen to and respect those whose position was less prestigious was often considered a weakness at best or a waste of time. This attitude prevailed both in the home and in business. All money – the symbol of power – was earned and budgeted primarily by husbands in a family setting. At work, the *boss* determined how assets were used… and few of them felt any need to give an account of the principles by which decisions were made. In such a setting, what need did one have for listening beyond the words spoken? Why would the 'little person' need to be understood when it was believed that what was needed in such a culture was a strong individual who could *talk*. When that rare husband or boss came along who listened with respect, those who lived or worked with such a leader felt blessed.

In our culture, we have not yet realized that such listening is not only a blessing, it is a requirement. Listening is an essential ingredient in human relationships. It is both a right and a gift…a gift that truly recognizes and honors another person. No wonder many never feel human! They have not been listened to as if they matter.

Today many people are struggling with one another, not because good relationships are impossible, but because we aren't willing to offer the understanding that comes with the listening skills that are so vital to human wholeness.

Present Needs

How does this attitude of struggling with one another affect us today? We are suffering! As pointed out previously, there are few villains in this struggle, just human beings without skills. We need a new way to look at life.

It is teamwork, not an aggressive authority or benevolent dictatorship, that is needed for human beings to become what we already are – *relational beings*. For this we need skills, clearly learned, carefully experienced, and consistently practiced.

Eventually, you may want to consider joining or organizing a support group in which you can practice the art of listening in a variety of dynamic situations that help you refine your listening skills.

$$\approx\!\!\sim$$

The ultimate goal of this program is to develop listeners who know how and when to skillfully accomplish the following:

1. Practice the roles of both listener and speaker.
2. Understand the difference between agreeing with and listening to others.
3. Know how to listen, not only with the mind, but also with the heart.
4. Recognize the stages we and others pass through because of the evolution of listening skills.
5. Communicate without defensiveness.

As you become more willing and able to be listener rather than speaker, and as you learn to put your own accumulated knowledge and ideas temporarily 'on the shelf,' these listening skills gradually become much more than 'techniques.' They become powerful assets that help you move smoothly along new pathways that change you and your experience of life! Learning to listen at the deeper levels of communication that are so necessary to human belonging is an *art* rather than a mere technique, and each of us develops our own artistry using these principles and tools.

Focused listening requires that someone, somewhere, be willing to listen rather than speak. It requires that the *learner/listener* establish an atmosphere of trust, openness, and acceptance rather than argumentation or control. Doing this changes the world.

It also changes *you* because the outcome of developing such a skillful art is the ability to hear without defensiveness, thus protective walls are no longer necessary and you begin to hear much more than you used to hear. Each speaker becomes your friend rather than your adversary. The communication becomes a two-way sharing instead of a battle of wits and ideas. Conflict, misunderstandings, and anger are avoided. Our past approach to family and business relationships can then move from an authoritarian structure of "I know more than you do," to one of cooperation and teamwork in which we share together what each of us knows for the good of all, including our relationships. Such a goal is not only required for good business and family peace, but absolutely essential for a full human life.

Where do we go from here? Looking at what was and what is can give us some sense of what will be. However, the future doesn't happen by accident. We make our future either by choice or by default. And we never make our future alone. We are in this together, and because we are partners in the creation of our future, we need to understand one another.

We need to stand before one another with a desire to honor and respect the future hopes and dreams of both ourselves and those with whom we walk through life at home, at work, and in society. As we offer others our own insights and experiences, we listen just as carefully and respectfully to theirs.

What can we do next? *We work toward transformation of our own desire to control or convince.* We create the moments in which we recognize

> *"Life has much mystery to it and so requires much trust, commitment, and giving of oneself without secure assurances of success or fulfillment.*
>
> *— Understanding*
> Charles A. Curran

another's wisdom and/or perception as well as our own. We rejoice when we learn to listen as well as speak. We gradually – or even quickly – let go of any fixed agenda or direction and begin to look for ways of hearing other possibilities. We begin to enjoy the expanded creative possibilities that show up when we start listening outside the box that we used to live in.

Once I was at a party where my mother, my sisters, and I were putting together a family banquet. One of my sisters handed me the salad ingredients and asked me to make a tossed salad. As I picked up the carrots, she began to tell me how to cut them. I could have become defensive and berated her for trying to control me or for treating me as if I did not know how to cut carrots. Instead I said, "There are lots of ways to cut carrots."

That was an important statement, which I still say both to myself and those with whom I live and work: "There are many ways to cut carrots!" The truth is, there are lots of ways to do anything!

Our lives together will have less conflict or need for control if we look at life as a mixed salad. What does it matter how one cuts carrots as long as they all go into the same bowl and are shared equally with everyone? Once we let go of the 'one right way' theory (usually my way!) we are ready for great adventures and wonderful discoveries. When we believe that everyone has the ability to cut carrots – no matter how they do it – our future will be not only peaceful but exciting!

SETTING THE STAGE

Because this book comes out of a personal experience of focused listening learned at a seminar called *The Art of Listening*, it will follow the process and content used in that seminar. *The process is primary.* The content has evolved as it was taught to various adult learners from many different professions and settings. As you begin to use this process, you will also create new ways of looking at the material. Hopefully, by the continued practice of the process, deeper clarity, understanding, and inner discoveries will also unfold for you.

The participants in the original seminars were primarily counselors and spiritual directors who had come to learn a new way to work with clients and spiritual seekers in ways that went beyond the methods studied in Psychology.

After World War II, Fr. Charles Curran, the creator of this method as well as our original presenter, felt that it was time for the 'age of science' to be superseded by what he called 'the age of the person.' Perhaps there would be fewer wars if we learned to really listen to one another from the heart. Curran had long realized that the goal of counseling and spiritual direction was to consider not only the mental dynamics involved, but also to help achieve movement in one's life through personal growth and change. Spiritual direction can take us beyond these goals to the full integration of the spiritual as well as the mental and emotional areas of our lives. We become fully mature humans who move through life with wisdom and grace.

Similarly, education saw as its goal intellectual growth and change through the imparting of knowledge. Although the purpose of both education and counseling/spiritual direction is *change*, the approach to each seemed to create divisions between the mind, the emotions, and the heart. *The Art of Listening Seminar* was developed as a way to integrate heart, mind, and soul.

Another challenge that also surfaced was the difference between teachers and students when adult learners began to return to the classroom. Because this new breed of students brought with them extensive experience and wisdom of their own, the instructor was no longer working with young minds and thus could no longer presume that all he or she had to do was impart new knowledge to a young mind. Because the teacher and students were *both knowers,* there was resistance in the learner which unfolded in different ways.

The content in the following chapters will deal with reasons for some of this resistance and how one might best handle it. The *process itself* will be consistent. This process will also be explained as we move through the reflections shared in the book.

Now take a moment to go through the questions for Reflection on the next page. Feel free to write your answers in the pages of this book.

REFLECTION QUESTIONS

SETTING THE STAGE

1. What are your early home and school memories of learning and growing up?

2. When did you recognize the importance of expressing both your insights and emotions?

3. Did you ever wonder how your religious and spiritual experiences were essential to the way you lived? When and how?

4. Who were some of your favorite teachers and why?

(Use the reverse side of the page if necessary)

ॐ

THE LISTENER'S CONTRACT

WHENEVER SOMEONE ASKS TO BE HEARD AND UNDERSTOOD, THE FOL-lowing contract is created between them:

> "I want to share something with you and I hope you will hear me and deeply understand me. I also hope you will not give me advice, nor be defensive, attacking, or sarcastic. Perhaps, most of all, I hope you have no agenda for me...but only unconditional love."

Sometimes this contract is spoken; sometimes it is just assumed. But for all of us, these are our deepest hopes in every relationship we share, especially with family and friends. For when these are present in the verbal exchange, we feel safe, appreciated, and understood.

Thus, when someone is speaking, this contract requires that you will actively respond as the listener, limiting your responses to:

* only the information you heard the speaker say
* only the feelings or emotion you pick up from the speaker
* only the images that come to you from the speaker's words and feelings

No personal ideas or questions are allowed when you are the listener!

YOU ARE PROBABLY FAMILIAR WITH
THESE KINDS OF CONVERSATION
AND COMMUNICATION...

Qualities Needed
for the
Art of Listening

&∽&

LISTENER:	SPEAKER:
1. A learner	1. A knower
2. Suspends judgment	2. Searching, clarifying
3. Understanding heart	3. Needs understanding
4. Respectful	4. Desires to be heard
5. Non-defensive	5. Desires to grow/change
6. Accepting	6. Wants to be responsible
7. Trustworthy	7. Wants to be open
8. Confidential	8. Wants to trust

DOODLE OR WRITE YOUR OWN PERSONAL THOUGHTS, NOTES, IDEAS, AND OBSERVATIONS HERE:

Course Outline of Day 1

༄༅

A Non-Abrasive Way to Relate

Morning

Different styles of communication

Difference between focused listening and ordinary communication

The difference between listening and giving advice

Roles of Speaker and Listener

Qualities of Listener (learner)
  Suspends judgment
  Caring & understanding heart
  Respectful
  Non-defensive
  Accepting
  Trustworthy
  Confidential

Qualities of Speaker (knower)
  A Knower, "giving birth to self"
  Searching, clarifying
  Needs understanding
  Desires to be heard
  Desires to grow & change
  Wants to be responsible
  Wants to trust

Structure Used in the Art of Listening

Afternoon

Belief systems as barriers
  Seeing life as 'laws and rules'
    Authority
    Right or wrong
    Judgment

Seeing life as 'relationships'
     Understanding
     Support
     Acceptance and trust

Unconscious and Non-Verbal dynamics involved
     Belief systems
     Unconscious blocks
     Attitudes toward power and community
     Past experiences

Physical and Psychological need to hear one's own words and feelings
     Helps clarify & sort out confusion within oneself
     Shows acceptance and care from the listener

Chapter 2

☙☙

A Non-Abrasive Way to Relate

Different Styles of Communication

The process of communication is many-faceted. Courses advertising 'communication techniques' include presentations, debate, discussion, questions, negotiation, convincing, argument, and dialogue as well as listening. Many of these styles of communication presume that we all speak the same language or are 'on the same page.' Regardless of style, we each speak from our own world, seldom realizing that our partner or audience may come from a radically different world view than ours, or has a far different experience of life, culture, values, or deep beliefs.

Because of these differences, our conversation frequently moves into argument, defense, or perhaps total withdrawal. Even as you read this you may remember times when this happened to you or you felt it coming from the reaction or silence of another. That awareness, either in yourself or another, is a red flag. It means you have moved from the surface, safe discussion about the weather or latest news report. You have now begun to touch the deeper places where you may radically differ in values, beliefs, or perceptions of life. When this happens, you have several choices to make. You can withdraw, change the subject, continue the conflict, or stop talking and move to an understanding mode of focused listening. This requires what I call 'dying to oneself so another might live.' In the language of the Art of Listening Seminar, it means that you become the *listener/learner* and you invite the other to become the *speaker/knower.*

One of my clearest memories of this 'dying to oneself' happened years ago when I was visiting my mother. I had learned the Art of Listening and was determined to practice it. I had a perfect chance when we both began to share our love for Scripture...and it turned into a debate, then a heated argument.

Our family was raised on a daily reading of the Bible, and at the time of my visit, my mother had a pattern of reading it daily for several hours. At that time also, I was teaching Scripture at one of the local colleges. I was sharing some of the content I was teaching at the time and my mother began to argue about it. That was a challenge for me! I considered myself a 'scholar' and wasn't about to quit the discussion.

My mother knew the Bible inside out, so she too was a knower/speaker and was also not about to quit telling me what she believed. I took a deep breath; I recognized we were getting pretty negative. I moved to a listening stance long enough to respond with words that would show an understanding of what she was sharing. By that simple – *not easy!* – act of letting go and dying to myself, we both moved from the *mind* to the *heart,* and I learned some deep insights into my mother's practical, earthy faith.

This story describes what I call a conversation with two speakers and no listeners. One of us had to die to herself, become the listener/learner, and let the other be the speaker/knower. That moment of listening is a precious memory for me even today as

I recall what I may have missed had I not stopped talking as the speaker/knower.

In *The Gift of a Listening Heart* you will learn to distinguish between each of the above. The primary goal will then become *focused listening*. Once you understand that skills other than listening are not your primary concern in this work, you will be able to plunge into the process, as well as the content, of this book.

REFLECTION QUESTIONS

DIFFERENT STYLES OF COMMUNICATION

1. How were differences in communication style and world views handled in your family and school?

2. Describe a time when you shut down because of the conflict caused by differences of opinion you had with others.

3. Who are the people in your life that you feel most in harmony with and why?

✑✑

LISTENING VS. GIVING ADVICE

Active listening is one of the tools used in counseling, guidance, and psychotherapy. Behavior modification, guidance, and advice-giving are other tools used in these fields. When seeking counseling, guidance, and/or psychotherapy, the clients often expect the 'expert' to tell them what to do. This expectation is detrimental to the client's own ability to make choices, see options, and recognize personal abilities and limitations.

The word *guidance* denotes a helpful skill when a client needs information for making choices. The word *counsel*, however, denotes true listening – a gift from the heart, and allows people to make their own choices by inviting them to discover their own inner resources. This is actually the meaning of the phrase 'to take counsel.'

The Hebrew word for 'counsel' means both listening and understanding. It is also the root word used for the gift of counsel. The Hebrew word for the gift of counsel comes from Solomon's prayer found in the Bible in the first book of Kings, Chapter three:

"Give your servant, O Lord, a listening heart…"

Because counselors and psychotherapists use both active listening and guidance, people sometimes confuse the 'gift of counsel' with giving advice. The skills of guidance, advice-giving, and behavior modification are *not* the purpose of this book or the course that this book is based on. These forms of counsel may be appropriate in other settings and effectively used by counselors or psychotherapists. However, our concern during this seminar is to

> *The Hebrew word for the gift of counsel comes from Solomon's prayer:*
> *"Give your servant, O Lord, a listening heart…"*
> 1 Kings 3

present *focused listening* – a style of listening that involves a two-step process:

1. To carefully and clearly understand the *speaker*.

2. To give a verbal response that will demonstrate to the *speaker* that he/she has been heard at both the cognitive (thinking) and the affective (feeling) level.

The Gift of a Listening Heart teaches us, through constant practice, to both understand and then verbally and skillfully reflect this understanding of another person, which is quite an art! To accomplish this, the book concentrates its content and practice on the ability to hear and understand what a person is *both feeling and thinking*. Through the modeling of skilled facilitators, participants learn and practice focused listening.

Focused listening trusts that people can recognize within their heart the choices that are most true to their own self when they are heard and the choices named by a skilled listener. A skilled listener who has listened to and trusted the deep spirit within themselves will also hear beyond the client's words to the desired, hopes, dreams, fears, and limits of a speaker, whether that is someone who comes for counseling and spiritual direction, or is a family member or friend that has a passion and hunger to grow and is in need of a listening heart.

Notice that there are requirements for both the client who speaks and the counselor who listens. Both must seek in their own life the kind of transformation essential to go beyond ego to what Thomas Merton calls 'the true self.' This is particularly true in what is sometimes called spiritual counseling.

Over the years, I have been blessed with spiritual directors who have put their finger on those places in me that are more ego than spirit. They have not judged me nor required a particular response under pain of sin or punishment. Because of this, I have been able to hear the truth without fear...perhaps with pain or disappointment, yes, but not fear. Fear leads to a fight or flight response and that is when most of us defend or withdraw for protection.

How many stories have we read in scripture about Jesus' approach to people who came to him with a deep hunger to grow and learn. The Samaritan woman at the well; Zacchaeus, the tax collector; or the blind man in Jericho often remind us of our own willingness to hear the raw parts of ourselves when we are listened to by an accepting, non-judging, and compassionate heart.

REFLECTION QUESTIONS

COUNSELING AND ADVICE-GIVING

1. As you read the request in the prayer of Solomon, did you think of anyone in your life who has that gift of counsel?

2. How do you react or respond when someone gives you advice? Why do you react that way?

3. Are there any people in your life who can – without attack or conflict – name the areas where you may need improvement? Are there any for whom you can do the same?

4. Read the following Scripture stories of Jesus and ask how he applied the principle of naming without attacking:
   * Woman taken in adultery (John 8:1-11)
   * Scribes and Pharisees (Matthew 23: 1-12)
   * Judas (Luke 22: 21-30)

፨

ROLES OF SPEAKER AND LISTENER

We have been reflecting on some of the styles of communication and looking at the ways in which we both speak and listen to one another. We have also discussed some of the professional skills used when people seek understanding so that they may better handle personal growth and emotional stability during difficult life events. In these reflections we have stressed the hopes, expectations, gifts, and limits of the client. But what about the hopes, expectations, gifts, and limits of those to whom clients, family, and friends go when they need someone to talk to?

What do counselors, professional caregivers, or family and friends need for themselves? In what ways do they seek personal growth?

My first experience in learning the art of listening was shared with others who were counselors, spiritual directors, and pastoral care professionals who, like myself, were ready to commit time and money to the seminar. We all set aside a full week (12 hours per day) to learn and practice this skill, which was advertised as an experiential workshop in which the content of the seminar would be integrated through group practice. Those who attended were immediately introduced to a clearly defined process.

> *"The first act of the self re-appraisal process, the taking of counsel, may be understood as self-research."*
>
> — *Understanding*
> Charles A Curran

Fr. Curran, the presenter, was the speaker. We, the participants were the active, responsive listeners. Specific qualities were presented for each of these two roles. And we were told very bluntly that if we stepped out of our roles as listeners and tried to become speakers, Curran would stop us and ask us to continue our response as listeners *only*. We agreed to follow this process, having no idea how many times we would be caught switching from listener to speaker!

At that time, I was living with another Sister who was unable to attend, but was eager to hear what I was learning. It was a perfect way to practice the skill of being a speaker to an interested listener. It was a true gift that we were able to share, and eventually we began to use the process in events that took place in our personal lives and would take turns being listener for each other.

Because of those experiences, I knew that focused listening could be effectively translated in every day situations. In order to accomplish that possibility, I continued to attend and help as facilitator for various listening seminars around the country. Eventually, we translated the presentations and the process into materials that could be applied in a variety of places: schools, hospitals, pastoral care centers, businesses, marriage counseling, churches, families, or any place where people or groups needed to communicate.

My passion to teach the process and write this present book comes partly from seeing the transformation that occurs when one is deeply listened to, and partly from the study of so many stories found in the gospels. Jesus freely shared his own deepest hopes, values, and beliefs with those willing to listen. He also easily became a sacred listener to those hoping for healing from fear, disease, or lack of direction and meaning in life.

I have had many powerful experiences of witnessing the personal transformation that happens when people are able to hear and be heard in the deepest part of their soul. One of the most profound memories I have is of a phone call I received a few years ago from the wife of a married couple who took the course in listening when the company they worked for offered it to management and their spouses. Bob and Mary were both so completely changed through the experience that they became facilitators for various other groups where the course was offered. They used it constantly with each other and often shared with groups the effect it had on their life together. The phone call came from Mary just one hour after she heard of the death of her husband, Bob, in a truck accident. She told me she needed to say how grateful she was because of their shared experience of listening with the heart. Her words were, "Bob and I may not have had as long a marriage as we had hoped for, but we know we became closer in the last two years than most couples experience in fifty."

REFLECTION QUESTIONS

ROLES OF SPEAKER/LISTENER

Reflect on the roles defined in this chapter and respond:

1. Have you ever gone to a professional counselor or spiritual director? What were your hopes and expectations? Did you continue to work with them? Why or why not?

2. What are the most important qualities you would look for...
   * in a speaker?
   * in a listener?

3. How have the following people in your life responded to your hopes and concerns?
   * Your parents
   * Spouses
   * Friends and co-workers

4. Describe the most recent situation in which you were able to put your own thoughts and attitudes 'on the shelf' and just listen.

҂∾҂

QUALITIES NEEDED FOR SPEAKER AND LISTENER

The roles of both listener and speaker are of equal importance in communication that is based on maintaining good relationships. An important question is: Which role – speaker or listener – initiates communication at all levels of understanding and clarity? We often consider the speaker as the initiator. This is true when there is a need for information alone. However, for a deeper understanding between two people, the *listener* initiates the process through acceptance, non-judgment, and a recognition that the speaker is the *knower* and the listener is the *learner*.

In such a process, one soon realizes that listening is an art and the listener is the artist who, through his or her own interior qualities creates a safe atmosphere in which both sharing and clarification can take place.

Why do we suggest that the listener is responsible for such an atmosphere? Why not the speaker? Each of us approaches most relationships carrying an assortment of past experiences of judgment or rejection, perhaps even personal attack or ridicule. We therefore fearfully and protectively tiptoe into one another's space. We are careful to share only that which is most safe – unimportant facts that we call 'small talk.'

The deepest parts of ourselves are hidden safely from the view of those who may hurt us. We have unique, unconscious protection systems that keep us from connecting and hinder deep and honest communication. This is not only true in casual relationships, but perhaps even more so in intimate ones such as friendship, marriage, and family. Who are the ones we fear to displease the most and why? Because of the many experiences of hurt between us, we often unconsciously need to protect ourselves. Such protection becomes a wall then, between ourselves and those we want most desperately to touch, reach, and become close to in life. Without realizing it at a conscious level, this need to protect becomes a defense mechanism which keeps people from knowing the most precious things about ourselves: our needs, hopes, fears, and dreams.

Because we often bring many of the above realities to each communication experience, let us repeat the qualities that are essential to one who wants to become a *focused listener*:

1. Non-judging mind
2. Listening heart
3. Attentive stance
4. Non-defensive attitude
5. Accepting spirit
6. Trustworthy/confidential commitment

Even as I write this, I think of how difficult it sometimes is to share these very thoughts with some of the most important people in my own life. Will they laugh at me? Some have in the past. Will they argue or debate? Will they sarcastically criticize my ideas or feelings? Will they walk away silently, uncaring, indifferent? When I teach 'The Art of Listening,' I share some of the deepest values and most intense feelings I have. What will you, the participant, do with them? Because I, as the present Speaker in this book, am the one who is opening myself up, sharing important feelings and ideas, I depend on you to receive then with respect and compassion. Will you do that? It is often such an unvoiced request that each speaker gives when they begin to talk to us in any setting.

People are hungry, often desperate, to be understood. Argument, debate, challenge, even some questions are not an understanding response. What is important to learn as a focused listener is a method or skill that will help you to respond to others with understanding only.

For this reason, I have seldom accepted questions or additional ideas during the live presentations given in my workshops. I am asking you only to understand. I, as presenter, will be the *speaker*. Facilitators are always present who will model the kinds of responses that lead to true understanding. As you get a sense of what an understanding response is, you are welcome to join the facilitators in the listening process.

Perhaps by now you are already aware that this style of learning is foreign to the usual style of listening/learning in our culture. We are used to questions, debate, competition, and argument as ways to arrive at 'truth.' *(See the graphic on Page 32.)* In past styles of learning, then, the one who could prove the most, or argue the best or loudest would often be the one who mattered the most and was most honored.

I would like to suggest that 'truth' lies within each of us no matter how quietly or unskillfully we talk. We are all both learners and knowers.

We each, in our personal life experiences, have acquired unique perceptions and a set of values upon which we have based our lives. We all have rare stories to tell one another. What I invite you to do in this course is listen to the stories, the values, and perceptions of each one who becomes a *speaker*. In doing so, keep in mind the following suggested qualities for the *speaker/searcher*:

1. One who both knows and is searching and clarifying
2. Needs understanding
3. Desires to be heard
4. Desires to change and grow
5. Desires to be responsible
6. Desires to be open and trusting

As you study the qualities listed for each role, notice that these qualities are more interior than exterior. This book and the listening course will help you learn to express them in an exterior way by practicing them through the listening process. In the beginning, it is important to understand that *we are not the role*. It is only a hat we wear on occasion.

However, I believe from years of working with people who are serious about using the gift of listening that there will be a continual change, not only in your listening ability but also in your trust and confidence that each of us has a piece of truth that we know and want to share. Through practice and learning to become a *focused listener*, these qualities will become who we are, not what we do.

We are all both learners and knowers. Through our personal life experiences, we have all acquired unique perceptions and a set of beliefs and values upon which we have based our lives. This course is, therefore, more focused on transforming your attitude than on teaching slick techniques. Technical skill will indeed come, but only as an outcome of an inner awareness that seeks to express itself and accept one another.

Reflection Questions

Qualities needed for the Speaker and Listener

1. Do you recognize any of these qualities in your own history or choices? Revisit Page 33 for the full list of qualities needed in a Speaker or Listener. Write down some qualities that would be important to you in a Speaker or Listener.

2. When you are with family and/or friends, which role do you prefer: Listener or Speaker? Why?

3. By necessity, we are often with people who are not safe. How have you protected yourself in the past when this happened to you? What are your methods of protection today?

4. Are there any other qualities you would add to the list for speaker or listener beyond what is described in this chapter? Why or why not?

ৡৢৡ

THE STRUCTURE USED IN
THE ART OF LISTENING

Lyman Coleman, creator of the Serendipity workshops, once said that the more firm the structure in group work, the freer will be the shared insights that surface. This has been true for the participants who were faithful to the structure designed for 'The Art of Listening' seminar.

It was indeed firm, clear, and consistent. The presentations were three hours long with a fifteen minute break in the middle. The *speaker* presented the content. The listening responses were modeled by trained facilitators who sat in four chairs, close to the speaker, and a small distance from the participants. The facilitators were introduced to the participants as 'models' of the process. As the participants began to understand the process, they were encouraged to become listening responders also.

It was the *speaker* who held the participants faithful to the 'listening responses only' model. Because the speaker was the knower, only he/she knew what they meant or felt in the presentations given. Therefore, only the *speaker* could know if he/she was being heard and truly understood. If the listener responded with their own ideas, feelings or experiences, it was the *speaker* who would say, "No, that isn't what I said. Tell me what I said...what did you hear?"

This was often the first struggle the listeners faced. Often we have no idea how many of our responses are about us, not about the speaker. Because the purpose of the process was to understand the speaker, dialogue, debate, personal insights, and corrections about the information were not accepted. If the listener continued by arguing or debate, we would then have two speakers. The process could not continue unless the listener was willing to let go of their own insights and return to the information and feelings being shared by the *speaker*. This was truly a 'dying to oneself.'

In this method of understanding, the burden is placed on the *listener* to 'die to self.' They need to remember that the speaker is on only one track – their own. But the listener has two tracks going on in his or her head: 1) the words and emotions of the speaker, and 2) the feelings, ideas, experiences, and reactions of their own. The personal thoughts of the listener do not have to be denied. They just need to be temporarily 'put on the shelf' while they are offering a listening heart to the speaker.

One good image for this model of listening is to be like a mirror, reflecting back to the speaker what you hear. The listeners are only 'reflectors,' showing in an understanding, supportive, compassionate way what is being offered by the speaker, without judgment, criticism, or additional information. As one becomes more skilled in this process, one may also hear what is not being said with words, but is clearly present as feelings, dreams, or values.

Carefully consider the Reflection questions on the next page. Then, in order to develop your skills and be faithful to this firm structure, we will move on to the next chapter to deeply consider the qualities needed for each of these roles of Speaker and Listener.

REFLECTION QUESTIONS

THE STRUCTURE USED IN THE ART OF LISTENING

Think about the structure used in focused listening and ask:

1. Who are the people in your life who listen to you without giving advice or adding their own story? What has been your reaction and response?

2. Think of the last time you experienced the death of a friend or family member. What did you say to those who were grieving? What did they say to you? How did it feel?

3. Is there anyone in your life with whom you can practice the art of listening? Why? Why not?

☙❧

DOODLE OR WRITE YOUR OWN PERSONAL THOUGHTS, NOTES, IDEAS, AND OBSERVATIONS HERE:

Chapter 3

ॐॐॐ

BELIEF SYSTEMS AS BARRIERS TO COMMUNICATION

PERHAPS ONE OF THE GREATEST BARRIERS TO COMMUNICATION is the belief that listening must involve *agreement*. One of the basic principles in the model of listening you will experience in this seminar is:

"I can hear you, understand you and support you as a person without agreeing with your ideas, values or beliefs. My own beliefs and values are not challenged or lost by developing a listening heart. I merely place them temporarily on the shelf while I attentively and actively hear *your* words and feelings."

This kind of total acceptance is quite rare. Our acceptance is usually reserved for those who agree with our values and opinions. If agreement or convincing is our goal, we will begin to argue, discuss, and debate rather than listen and understand. If we are able to *separate the person from the information, we will be less likely to judge or criticize.* We are then able to hear another person no matter how we might differ in our own understanding, information, insights, or values.

However, as one begins to listen to, understand, respect, and accept the person who is speaking, the *speaker* often feels like it is agreement! This is not always so, and this became very clear to me not long ago when one of our sisters shared this story:

An employee at Mary's place of business came into her office to talk about a work conflict. Mary listened compassionately, gave only listening-quality responses, and skillfully picked up the employee's feelings. Mary felt good about her ability to understand without judgment.

However, the next day the boss called Mary in and asked why she was taking sides with one of the employees when the conflict had created a very delicate situation. What Mary discovered was that when the employee went in to challenge the boss she said, "I talked this over with Mary and she agrees with me." In some situations, one needs to be clear and up-front about the difference between *listening* and agreement!

The idea that *listening* constitutes agreement as recounted in the story above comes from the way one looks at life. Some people see life as a hierarchy with an all-important authority figure at the top, and strict laws of right or wrong, good or bad. They think those who do not stay on the right side of the law deserve judgment and punishment.

Other people see life as a set of relationships that are based on understanding and trust. They feel that these relationships are more or less comfortable based on the amount of acceptance and support that is given and received among them.

The following may help explain how belief systems can be barriers as well as foundations for your life:

Seeing Life as:

Laws/Rules	Relationship
Authority	Understanding
Right/Wrong	Support
Judgment	Acceptance/Trust

LIFE AS LAWS AND RULES

If one sees a good and successful life as dependent on unchanging laws and absolute rules – all of which are decided by someone else outside the self, the model of learning and living becomes a matter of good or bad, true or false. Authority and proof become necessary for every decision. Judgments must be made on the basis of how accurate the *speaker's* ideas and/or feelings are. Someone has to be 'right' and the other one 'wrong.' Out of this belief system comes argument, challenge, questions, and debate. When there is only right or wrong, who wants to be wrong? A conclusion of seeing the world this way is that the person who does not argue with you must be agreeing with you!

There is a place for laws and rules. When it comes to scientific measurement and mathematical fact, laws and rules provide the premises on which to build a foundation. However, true scientists are constantly questioning the certitudes of the past. A world view based on laws and rules may be a good base for the study of math and science, however, let us not make such a system the final arbiter of what goes on in the human being.

In the raising of children, boundaries and limitations must be set. Wise parents and teachers do not demand exactly the same behaviors, attitudes, and understanding from each child. As children grow and develop, value systems and clear parental/teacher guidance through both modeling and teaching are vital to later adult decision-making.

When one becomes determined to impose absolute, unchangeable laws and rules to all of life, it becomes difficult to recognize a Galileo who sees beyond the human eye, or recognize a Columbus who risks his life on the roundness of an earth that appears so flat! It was this unbending mentality of laws and rules that would exist 'absolutely and forever' that made it impossible for some of the religious leaders to hear the new insights taught by Jesus of Nazareth.

Life may HAVE laws and rules…but that is not what life IS. There is another system that you are invited to embrace, one based on cooperation and love… *life as relationship*.

LIFE AS RELATIONSHIP

It was Jesus of Nazareth who said, "People were not made for the law; the law was made for people."

When you base your model of learning on people, human qualities are needed – not 'proof.' Rather than authority, you look for acceptance and trust; rather than right or wrong, you look for understanding and support. In this modality, each person's perception is honored. By sharing our values with one another without an agenda or territorial demands, something greater than each of us is discovered. There comes from within us a deeper truth than any of us has alone. I believe it is this experience of which John speaks when he wrote:

> "As for you, the anointing you received from Him remains in your hearts. This mean you have no need for anyone to teach you. Rather, His anointing teaches you…"
>
> *1 John 2:27*

In this scripture quotation, the word *you* is plural. This 'anointing' was what the early Christians called the presence of the Holy Spirit operating within the community. This inner truth is also available to us today as we gather 'two or three together' in God's name. To gather in our own name, with our own agenda and our own ego does not allow us to *draw from* this universal storehouse of truth.

As we seek to operate within a relationship model rather than the model of laws and rules, there are specific qualities that will be needed:

    Acceptance
    Trust
    Understanding
    Support for each of us as persons

You will recall that these are the qualities of the *listeners* (not of the *speaker*). When these qualities are missing from your response, I will let you know. I will not ask for agreement or disagreement of our ideas or feelings; only for *understanding* of them. Through the verbal response of the facilitators, you will begin to get a feel for the process. And again, I invite you also to respond as you become more clear about your role as *listeners*.

Reflection Questions

Belief Systems as Barriers
in Communication

1. As you read this chapter, what mode of operation do you feel is
   strongest in you:
   * Laws and rules?
   * Relationships?
   * Why do you feel this way, or why not?

2. How have you experienced the beliefs and values described in this
   chapter? How do you think those close to you operate regarding
   these beliefs and values?

3. When have you felt totally accepted and trusted by another? When
   have you been able to give that trust and acceptance to someone
   else in your life?

4. As you read the Gospels, what are some of your favorite stories in
   which Jesus demonstrated the *Relational* style...or the *Laws and
   Rules* style described in this chapter?

❧

Unconscious and Non-Verbal Dynamics

This belief in laws and rules or in relationship as the basis of communication that we described earlier does not always operate consciously. These are often hidden beliefs and values collected through the years and we act them out without awareness. Even when we are somewhat aware of them, we seldom verbalize the beliefs we hold. Because of this, there are subtle dynamics going on between us and within us that might be helpful to discuss.

In our live seminars there are people from all walks of life and from various genetic and generic backgrounds. Sex, race, work, and life styles all differ. The variety of life experiences, number of siblings, kinds of parenting, and influences of various teachers affect us in different ways. Such differences can help or hinder us from hearing and understanding one another. What you might say to me as an affirmation statement could be heard as an accusation. These are like hot buttons that accidentally get pushed when there are hidden agendas or unconscious dynamics going on in situations where we are trying to communicate.

An example: You may have entered this room expecting me to understand you. Your past experiences of 'teachers' may have been formed by those who created an atmosphere in which you (the learner) may or may not have been comfortable. So when I ask you to understand me, to make ME comfortable, you may well feel anger rising in you. This anger could create resistance to learning from me.

Another example: You may have been raised to ask questions and to debate. You have learned a great deal from questioning and arguing, and have appreciated the knowledge that has come from that style of learning. Therefore, when I say, "No questions," it doesn't make any sense to you! I have, by one statement, touched a button in you that creates an immediate wall between us.

Or: You have had very dominating teachers in your past, people who have not allowed you to participate or comment. You were forced to 'swallow' everything they said and later to regurgitate it on exams. So, when I say, "I am the only speaker and you must listen. Tell me only what you hear," memories of those harsh moments in your past block you from hearing any more of my words.

Or: You may have been taught that adults are always the authority. Some common advice given to many of us has been, "Children should be seen and not heard." Other statements to children include, "Never interrupt anyone! Do what I say, not what I do!"

These quotes are buried deep within many of us. Therefore, when I say, "Everyone is both knower and learner, no matter what our age," it doesn't match these inner, early directives that have made deep impressions on us.

> "...we have attempted to expose something of the inner dynamics of persons as they move, through being understood, toward more... control of those confusions and conflicts within the self that cause them self-defeat."
>
> — *Understanding*
> Charles A. Curran

The above stories are examples of belief systems, unconscious blocks, past experiences, and attitudes toward power and community that affect the dynamics between us. We all – both *listeners* and *speakers* – bring non-verbal and unconscious memories to our communication exchanges.

You may resist or embrace some of what you hear, not because it is right or wrong, but because it fits or doesn't fit what has been programmed within you from the past. That is why I say, "You do not have to agree with me... you only have to understand me." The insights I offer in this workshop are for your consideration. Feel them, think about them, try them, and then toss them out later if they don't work. Notice I say, *later*. While you are here, I will ask you to stay within the *listening format*. We will practice, practice, practice both in this large group and in smaller groups. During the small group sessions, you will each have time to be both *speaker* and *listener*. The facilitators will work with the small groups to help with the process. There will be opportunities after the small groups and during the breaks for questions or clarification from either the presenter or the facilitators.

REFLECTION QUESTIONS

UNCONSCIOUS AND NON-VERBAL DYNAMICS

Re-read the scenarios described in this section and ask yourself:
1. Which sample scenario is most true to my own experiences? Add any others you may also have experienced.

2. How did I feel about them during my early years?

3. Which of these scenarios do I continue to live and believe in to-day?

4. If I have changed my beliefs over the years, what have I learned or experienced that created the changes?

5. In which relationships have I refused to listen because I have be-lieved that 'to listen' is to agree? How could I shift my approach?

⊱⊰

Physical and Psychological Need to Hear One's Own Words and Feelings

The style of listening that is presented in *The Gift of a Listening Heart* is often called 'active listening.' It is active in the sense that the listener does not simply listen, he or she also gives a *listening response*. The response is, however, far more than mere repetition! As one learns to hear not only the words spoken, but also the feelings and struggles beneath the words, the verbal response becomes a gift: the willingness to walk with another without judgment.

This gift is vital to the *speaker*. He or she is often confused, uncertain, perhaps even embarrassed as feelings, struggles, and beliefs are deeply shared. It is imperative that the *speaker* feels support in the process. Our verbal responses, which capture the feelings, the insights, and the information of the *speaker* are essential to the process. A silent *listener* may be physically present, but it is only in the total unconditional listening response that the *speaker* knows he or she is connected with the *listener* and understood at both the affective and cognitive levels.

If you are a participant in one of the live presentations, you have either heard the facilitators giving me a verbal response, or you have heard my own plea, "Tell me what you heard." Or I may have asked you, "Does that make sense" or "Do you understand what I'm saying?"

All of the above questions are coming from *my need to be understood*. A silent smile or nod of the head is somewhat helpful, but they don't tell me anything! For all I know, your mind is somewhere in Tahiti.

The only way a *speaker physically* knows if you are totally, consciously, supportively with him or her is if you give an understanding response. This response is most helpful when it includes both the insights and information you heard, as well as the feelings you picked up from the *speaker*. Without this verbal response, you, as *listener*, could just as easily be replaced by a mirror or a tape recorder.

This need to be heard is both psychological and physical. We've already said that the *speaker* may feel embarrassed, confused, uncertain. To hear an unconditional, supportive response is very affirming when one isn't sure if his or her remarks even make sense!

This affirmation and acceptance affects the *speaker* even beyond the spiritual and psychological value mentioned above. Hopefully by now, you, too, especially if you are part of a live seminar, have felt the spiritual and psychological relief that comes from being heard and understood.

When I say, "Hopefully you have felt..." I am speaking of a neurological as well as a psychological effect that takes place in the process of being heard and understood.

We have found in our experiences of teaching the *Gift of a Listening Heart* seminar, that many participants sense a physical difference within their bodies when they are heard at all levels. We might suggest a kind of psychic connection between the cortex of the brain and the hypothalamus, where the emotional center seems to operate. This connection is what operates when a person's ears pick up the sound of his or her own words and/or feelings and direct it to the cortex of the brain.

The following diagram may describe this process better than words can...

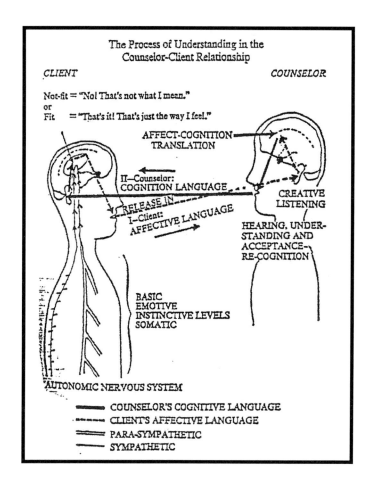

THE PROCESS OF UNDERSTANDING IN THE COUNSELOR-CLIENT RELATIONSHIP

This diagram is taken from the book *Understanding: An Essential Ingredient in Human Belonging* by Charles A. Curran, Ph.D. It uses the language of the counselor-client relationship to describe what happens both physically and psychologically.

In the diagram, the client (*speaker*) approaches the counselor (*listener*) with a desire to be understood. The *speaker*, however, may not yet understand exactly what his is looking for.

Often, in our conversations with one another, we are searching, struggling, and not always sure of our words or ideas. The diagram shows the dynamics that go on in such a struggle: the words come from the *speaker's* mouth into the *listener's* ear.

The *listener*, using an objective, creative process, allows his or her brain to formulate and offer words that the *speaker* can then hear and grasp. In this 'personal hearing' the *speaker* will recognize if the words spoken have, or have not, captured the basic meaning of his or her original conversation. If the *listener* is using all the qualities we spoke about in our first session, the *speaker* is then able to comfortably say: "Yes, that fits" or "No, that isn't what I meant."

It is in this step of the process when the *speaker* hears, recognizes, and confirms his or her own words, that the *speaker's* autonomic nervous system begins to relax. The *speaker's* desire to be both heard and understood, without judgment or attack, has been honored by the *listener*. In this experience of being truly understood, not just handed a nod, a smile, or a mumbled "uh-huh," that a feeling of relief takes place. Out of that instinctive relief comes an inner clarity that allows the *speaker* to understand, appreciate, trust, and respect himself or herself. We will continue to discuss this process in greater detail through the rest of the book.

Doodle or Write Your Own Personal Thoughts, Notes, Ideas, and Observations here:

Course Outline of Day 2

෨෬

BELONGING AND THE STAGES OF LEARNING

Morning

Brief Encounter and Focused Listening
    Affective content
    Cognitive content
    Values and Beliefs
Brief Encounter Form
Stages of Learning
    Stage 1 - Dependency
    Stage 2 - Opening to Learning
    Stage 3 - Navigating Ambiguity
    Stage 4 - Fine-tuning and Understanding
    Stage 5 - Interdependence
Personal Stance in the Communication Process
    Standing for
    Understanding
    Overstanding
Confusion
Defensiveness
Control
Manipulation
ReGroup

Afternoon

Cultural Inheritance
    Power vs. community
Scientific model
      Dichotomized person
Psychological model
    Categories

Mathematical model
    Analysis
    Problem-solving
    Role of questioning or doubt
New paradigm: key moments

Chapter 4

࿇

BELONGING AND
THE STAGES OF LEARNING

WE HAVE DESCRIBED THE PURPOSE, PROCESS AND STRUCTURE of the listening model. We have also pointed out some of the communication styles, personal qualities, and belief systems of both the speaker and the listener. Because of the differences each of us bring to the experience we call life, we have also suggested some of the possible conflicts these differences create.

Now I would like to invite you to consider some ways to transform these conflicts into a *relational* way of understanding one another as both a skill and a way of life. Our first requirement is to go beyond listening to a deep hearing and understanding of one another with both head and heart. The Art of Listening as presented here is not so much active as contemplative. We are asking you to hear with an 'inner ear,' the ear of the soul.

This affirmation and acceptance, clearly offered through the mirroring of the speaker's feelings and ideas, affects the speaker even beyond the physical and psychological value mentioned above. It also puts order into the words which, because of the speaker's possible inner uncertainty, often come out somewhat cluttered. When the speaker hears the orderly verbal response from an objective listener, that is when the neurological as well as psychological effect takes place in the process of being heard and understood.

Again, it is in this step of the process – the speaker's hearing, recognizing, and confirming his or her own words – that the speaker's autonomic nervous system begins to relax.

૭∾৶

> *"The end goal of all under-standing is human belonging."*
> — Charles A. Curran

The Brief Encounter and Focused Listening

We have already considered the difference between *counseling* and *advice-giving*. We know there may be times when a person is asking, perhaps not for advice, but for information. This is appropriate if one is asking for directions or for facts such as a specific answer to a math problem. There are many situations, however, when a person is asking for something deeper. These are times when external knowledge and facts are not enough.

Life has frequent moments in which someone (as the *speaker*) is trying to understand himself or herself. Perhaps they are trying to come to terms with a decision, a situation, relationship, etc. and thereby attain some inner peace. They just need someone to listen to them for a few minutes.

It is at moments like this that what I refer to as a "Brief Encounter" can be very helpful. The brief encounter includes the following:

1. Affective (how someone feels)
2. Cognitive (what someone knows)
3. Values, beliefs, etc. they hold as important

A brief encounter is a short but focused period during which a *listener* will give a specific period of time to a *speaker*. I am not suggesting the professional counselor's 50-minute hour. **The time suggested for a brief encounter is about ten minutes.** It could be a little more or a little less, but time is not as important as the willingness to be totally attentive for a short time, the duration of which should be set *before* the listening begins.

The word *brief* is a key word in this encounter. You can even set up a verbal contract or agreement that has a particular time limit. This can be important not only for you but for the speaker. Why? Have you ever noticed that there are some people who, if you say you have two hours, will take that entire amount of time?

Listening during the Brief Encounter is *not* offered to someone so that you can do all *their* inner work. It is offered so they have a way of getting 'unstuck,' enough so that they can go on with their life. Your purpose as a *listener* is not to solve their problem (although that may happen), but rather to be with the *speaker* in a caring, accepting way. Remember, one of the main goals of the listening process is to foster a sense of 'belonging' in the speaker.

To accomplish this, the *listener* needs to enter into the *speaker's* inner world without judgment, and to understand that world as it is perceived, felt, evaluated, and acted upon by the *speaker*. This requires an awareness so focused and sensitive that the *listener* is able to hear not only the conscious struggle, but the unconscious one as well. Thus, for a short time, the *listener* joins another human being in their journey.

As a spiritual director and counselor, I often give my phone number to people with whom I work. But it always comes with the sentence, "Ten minutes on the phone can get you through the night." Seldom have people taken advantage of me when I say this. I even have some who will call and say, "I think I only need five minutes." If the ten minutes doesn't seem to be enough, I will say, "It sounds like you need more time for this. Let's set up another time in the office."

These suggestions are really important because no one owns anyone's time or attention. No matter how skilled we might be or even how willing we are to spend more time, the Brief Encounter is not the time for lengthy therapy. Dependency is never healthy, but a good friend in time of need is a treasure.

There are many times we fail to listen to someone because we think we don't have time. More time does not necessarily guarantee the kind of listening we have been talking about in this book! In the Brief Encounter, I am talking about *quality time*, which requires the ability to put our own feelings and ideas aside and to concentrate on the person who may have quietly said to us: "I'd like to talk to you sometime."

Using the skills you are learning in this seminar will allow you as the *listener* to hear, understand, and verbally reflect the words of the *speaker* at two levels: the cognitive (thoughts, ideas, insights) and the affective (feelings, beliefs, and values).

As you become more skilled at being a good *listener* through the kind of practice we are doing here (both in the large and small groups), your ability to do focused listening will become a natural response during any conversation – short or long.

If you are part of one of the live seminars, we would like to demonstrate this process for you right after our next break. In order to do it, I will ask for two volunteers. One would be willing to share a negative emotion or situation for about ten minutes. The second would discuss a positive emotion or situation. During that time, I will carefully listen to each one, and reflect what I hear. You, as the group, will also have a chance to listen just as carefully to each volunteer *speaker*. Formulate your own possible responses and see how they compare to the ones I give. Watch my timing, expression, and words as well as feelings, ideas, and insights. Notice the *speaker's* responses. You (the group) will be participant observers. I will be the *listener* and let each volunteer know when the time is about finished. This is not role-playing. It will be real and hopefully enriching for both the volunteers and you as a group.

THE BRIEF ENCOUNTER FORM
TO BE USED BY THE LISTENER
WHEN WORKING WITH A SPEAKER

Pay attention to the need and the style of the Speaker, as well as his or her reasons for requesting that someone listen.

Contract for the Brief Encounter:

1. Listen for clues that the person needs a listener.

a) Give a listening response that recognizes both information and feelings.

b) Listen to the speaker's response and the level of trust, openness, and desire to clarify and grow.

2. Listen for the reasons behind the request for a listener.

a) Desire to be understood

b) Needs to clarify; desires trust

c) Desires to be connected to the listener

d) Wants to be knower/preacher/teacher

e) Wants an audience, not an 'understander'

f) No desire to clarify or search deeper (stuck)

g) Problem-solving or advice

h) Wants to vent feelings

3. Monitor the dynamics of your response as a listener.

a) Maintain a balance of facts and feelings

b) Use good images to combine the two

c) Be aware of unconscious elements within yourself (beliefs, traditions, values, etc.)

d) Be aware of areas of defensiveness within yourself

e) Be aware of resistance within yourself because of disagreement

f) Be aware of wanting to add your own information, stories, and experiences

g) Maintain a willingness to put yourself and your own ideas, beliefs, etc. 'on the shelf'

4. **Listen and watch for movement toward another style of communication** (See the graphic 'Circle of Communication' on pg. 32)

a) Can you or the speaker add to the conversation when you agree?

b) Are you naming things and clarifying issues when you differ?

c) Can you negotiate when you need to decide?

d) Are you giving information when needed?

e) Are you giving guidance or options when appropriate?

f) Are you offering appropriate challenges or questions when invited?

The Stages of Learning

"No one understands me!"

Deep understanding is such a common hunger among all of us! Yet it seems to be the least available commodity in the world today. We are often not understood, or we do not understand. This is seldom a deliberate response. Rather it comes from confusion or expectation. The people involved in a conversation are not always sure who is the one being understood and who is the one expected to understand. Therefore, what often began as a wonderful conversation ends with confusion and perhaps hurt. The questions I will raise here are *Why?* and *What can we do about it?*

In these scenarios, we will shift our use of terms a little. Instead of using the terms *speaker* and *listener*, we will use the terms *knower* and *learner*. The *knower* is the one who knows what he or she is trying to share or teach. The *learner* is the one who is learning to grow and develop himself, or perhaps is learning a process or skill.

In every situation of communication, there is a *knower* and a *learner*. Reflect on the following scenarios and determine who is the *knower* and who is the *learner*:

- We are working on a project and we get 'stuck' in the middle of the page of directions. We look for someone who can help us untangle the confusion.

- A mother is fixing a meal in the kitchen and a child comes in wanting to help.

- A student enters first grade and has been waiting for years to learn how to read. The teacher is the magic *knower* who can make that happen.

- A daughter has just learned a new dessert recipe and wants to share it with her mother.

· A son is involved in an electronics class in school. He is excited about some new insights and wants to discuss them with his father.

How does the *knower* pass on their valued information to the *learner*? First, we need to recognize that the *learner*, especially when he or she is young, comes with some hesitancy, fear of failure, or perhaps concern that he or she might not be accepted and encouraged. When the *learner* is attempting to learn something new and knows very little about it (whatever it is), the *knower* is often extra patient and encouraging. This can be considered stage one in the learning process.

Perhaps the best example of this is the parent helping a child to talk. The parent often accepts any word, or even any sound that resembles a word, when a child is first struggling to accumulate a vocabulary. However, as the child grows older and more competent with language, the parent begins to correct certain pronunciations and is not quite so patient and accepting.

If we look closely at each of the above scenarios, we will discover that this desire to be understood operates at all ages. We may also recognize in each situation that whether we are referring to the position of *knower* or the *learner*, there is no special age requirement for either. A four-year-old can be the *knower* and a grandparent can be the *learner*. However, in the early stages of development, it is often the younger one who is the *learner*, and as we grow older, we more often want to be recognized as a *knower*. It is this need to be a *knower* that creates so many conflicts in communication involving all age levels.

My father was a very patient teacher with all of us, but my favorite story was one my mother told me long after his death. She came from a farm family in the south where few of the girls went past the eighth grade.

My father's entire family was well-educated. My paternal grandfather was from Europe and could speak four or five languages fluently. After my parents were married, my father and mother frequently attended dinners involving my father's business. My mother told me that he would memorize the words or grammar she mispronounced and when they came home, he would teach her how to say them. But he never corrected her in public. For my father, her feelings were more important than the impression it would make on others.

That story continues to remind me that in some areas all of us might be at stage one in the learning cycle. And all of us can learn to be the kind of understanding teacher that my father was. Perhaps one of the reasons it is difficult to learn as adults is because we have been embarrassed in early years by impatient parents or teachers. Understanding the stages of the learning process combined with the skills of listening can be very helpful in deciding when to be a *knower* and when to be a *learner*.

> *"There is a philosophical axiom, the origin of which is lost in time, which states that no learning takes place outside of a love relationship... Learning happens between persons. Knowledge does not exist in some space...it exists among us."*
>
> — *Education in a New Dimension*
> J. Rardin and D. Tranel

As you study the following stages, remember that *understanding* is the most important quality in the process of learning. Please notice in each of the following *Stages of Learning* **who** is the one required to understand in order for learning to take place with safety and trust. These stages show the conflicts that arise throughout the full knowing-learning process on both sides.

The Five Stages of Learning in the Listening Process:

STAGE 1 - Dependency

a) The *knower* is the one who offers to listen and understand someone. The *knower* enters into a contract relationship with the *learner*.

b) The *learner* is dependent on the one who knows. He needs understanding, information, and the ability to think for himself.

STAGE 2 - Opening To Learning

a) The *knower* encourages the *learner* to pay attention to his or her own words and feelings, as well as responses to the things the knower says and does. The *knower* continues to understand and listen while encouraging the *learner* to move toward greater awareness and independent thinking.

b) The *learner* opens to understand self and the world, and begins to move toward the independent thinking that will allow him to organize his thoughts and feelings in a more mature and effective way.

STAGE 3 - Navigating Ambiguity

In this stage, both individuals want to be *knowers* and it becomes the responsibility of the *knower* to recognize that the *learner* is beginning to know things for himself. This stage is very delicate and important for, if they are not careful, a power struggle can begin as the roles of *knower* and *learner* shift back and forth between them. At times, each must maintain a dual role as both *knower* and *learner*.

a) The *knower* must recognize that the *learner* is becoming a *knower* who is beginning to know himself at deeper and deeper levels. The *knower* must therefore shift when appropriate to become a *learner* who is learning about this newly emerging individual.

b) The *learner* wants to be recognized as a *knower* and struggles to assert himself as such. However, the *learner* can move unexpectedly between being a *knower* and a *learner*. He also needs more information and the wisdom of experience before he will stabilize as a good *knower* in his own right.

STAGE 4 - Fine-tuning & Understanding

In this stage, the process is ongoing, with the *learner* spending more and more time as a *knower*.

a) The *knower* continues to listen and to encourage the *learner* to gain wisdom and perspective. The *knower* continues to demonstrate the qualities of a good listener so the *learner* will continue to learn and develop the ability to listen and move into greater maturity, wisdom, and understanding.

b) The *learner* fine-tunes his knowledge and begins to offer listening and understanding to others.

STAGE 5 - Interdependence

In the culmination of a successful listening process, the *knower* and *learner* may begin to collaborate with one another to nurture further growth in each other as they move fluidly back and forth between the roles of *knower* and *learner*.

a) The *knower* enjoys interdependence and dialogue with the new knower.

b) The *learner* becomes a *knower* who is able to listen to others, offer understanding, and who now works interdependently with others.

Let's look at these five stages a little more deeply. In the first stage, the *learner* is totally dependent on the *knower* for understanding and acceptance. The *knower* is the one who is required to set the atmosphere for trust and non-judgment. The *knower* in this first stage is both the understander and the *knower*. It is, therefore, the *knower* who must have the following qualities right from the start:

1. No judgment
2. A caring attitude
3. A listening heart
4. Non-defensiveness
5. Acceptance of the other
6. Trustworthiness in the self

The purpose and hope of the *knower* is to help the *learner* become less dependent, less manipulated or controlled, more mature and more able to recognize and sort through the conflicts in himself.

In the second stage, the *knower* continues to listen and understand, while also encouraging independence, clarity, and acceptance when the *learner* is truly honest with himself and is willing to look at who he really is and how he feels and thinks. The *learner* then gradually accumulates more and more of the information and perspective taught by the *knower*. Regardless of how painful this stage might be for the *learner*, this is a real growth period for him.

As the *learner* becomes more of a *knower*, he begins to exercise independence in various ways. Throughout this stage, the *knower* must continue to express understanding qualities. In this way, the *learner* can be gradually led to make better personal decisions and also be affirmed when he begins to operate as a *knower*.

By Stage 3, the *learner* is beginning to know that he no longer wants to be controlled. At this stage there is a great deal of ambiguity between the *learner* and the *knower*.

This is a key point in the process... *The learner begins to know much of what the knower knows, and because most learners are still too inexperienced to be wise and patient in their own learning process, a real struggle may take place between the learner and the knower.*

Now they are both *knowers*...and the question arises, *Are they both willing to be learners as well?*

It is at Stage 3 and beyond in the learning process that the responsibility for offering understanding qualities extends not only from *knower* to *learner,* but from *learner* to *knower*. Only if the *learner* is now willing to become caring, understanding, and non-judgmental will the *knower* be able to continue teaching without conflict.

If the *learner* can open deeply enough that he takes a position of being non-judgmental, allows himself to care, begins to listen with an open heart having full acceptance and no defensiveness, he can move from Stage 3 to Stage 4 of the process. He must now also be one who willingly chooses to understand.

When this happens, the *learner* can then acquire further depth and insight. He will begin the fine-tuning that leads to wisdom that only the *knower* can give.

Stage 5, then, is the one in which, through personal humility and transformation, respect and trust, the disciple becomes the master. The *learner* (originally the disciple) becomes the *knower* and is now master of his life. He has, by his own inner transformation, created an atmosphere in which there is no arrogance or competition. Thus, *interdependence* becomes the bond that unites both *knower* and *learner*. They have successfully navigated the stages of learning!

An excellent example of these stages of learning can be found in the parenting process. In Stages 1 and 2, parents – the *knowers* – raise their child who is the *learner*. They recognize the child's need to become a mature, fully functional, balanced adult.

As the child learns and grows, the relationship enters Stage 3 where there is a real struggle because now both parents and teen are *knowers*. It is at this time that the parents must be willing to become *learners*. Who is this newly emerging adult they have raised? The parents not only have to evaluate their success so far in bringing their child to maturity, they must continue to walk with that child as the child uses what he knows, practices making decisions, and learns to listen to others.

If parents and teen can get through this stage, they will enter Stage 4 where a great deal of depth and insight is gained, along with experience and a mature power. The parents must continue to offer guidance, acceptance, and love as they trust in the child and his ability to become all that he can be. This then leads to Stage 5 when parents and child become interdependent friends, and the parents can relax and step back knowing they have raised a competent, well-balanced human to help carry on the world.

Another example of such a process is the relationship that developed between Jesus of Nazareth and his disciples. Their early dependence upon Jesus was met with his patience and understanding. Gradually, Jesus invited them to use what he had taught them. The story of the multiplication of the loaves and fishes is a fine example. The disciples told Jesus that the people were hungry and Jesus said, "Feed them yourselves." He was inviting them to use some of the spiritual power he had already modeled.

In yet another example, Jesus had gone from town to town, healing and teaching, once again modeling for the disciples what was also to be their ministry. Eventually, Jesus sent the disciples from town to town, two by two. Interestingly enough, he didn't go along! He waited until they returned and then listened to their stories of all the wondrous events that had happened.

As the disciples told Jesus their stories, they also asked how to solve some problems which they had encountered. As he refined their knowledge and practice, they learned more, until the day when Jesus left them altogether. He trusted by then that they had what they needed to complete the work that he, the master, had begun. The disciples had gone through joy and pain, struggle and trust, even fears and failures, to learn the lessons they needed in order to know what Jesus knew. Only the disciple who is able to walk in a master's footsteps will truly learn all that the master has to offer.

PERSONAL STANCE IN THE COMMUNICATION PROCESS

Each of us approaches the process of communication with our own personal values, beliefs, and/or attitudes. When we are the *speaker*, no matter how objective we may try to be, our information, insights, and feelings are always influenced by these values and beliefs.

When we want to share these with another, we are 'taking a stand' or 'standing for' something very personal. When the other person is listening, many times the *listener* finds herself reacting either negatively or positively to the *speaker's* words and feelings. This reaction is not coming from the fact that the *speaker* is good or bad, right or wrong. It is happening because it sounds like the *listener's* personal stance is being affirmed or denied. The *speaker* is touching something very personal in the *listener.*

If a *speaker* seems to deny a belief that is very precious to us, we often become argumentative, defensive, or angry. Perhaps we may even cry. These are natural reactions when we are personally invested and care deeply for the speaker and the ideas or beliefs he/she may be sharing.

These are the dynamics that make it very difficult to apply the qualities that we ask for from a good *listener.* How can one understand when one is busy standing for something instead of listening?

The following outline may help clarify the process I will now describe:

1. Standing for
2. Understanding
3. Overstanding
    a. Confusion
    b. Defensiveness
    c. Control
    d. Manipulation
    e. Other…

As Charles Curran pointed out in his book *Understanding,* the important word in the above list is *stand.* If 'to stand for' something is to commit to it, then to *understand* something is to 'get under' a stand, to get to the root of a stand, or perhaps to enter into the world of a learner in order to know what sorts of conflicts and sorrows or joys and satisfactions they are experiencing so you can be of help and they can let go of any pain or conflict.

Similarly, to *overstand* is to take a stand in which the knower tries to assume power over someone in order to quickly resolve a problem or brush away an issue. The one who overstands means well, but when you try to push your answers onto someone else, you create resistance.

SCENARIO:

A good friend of yours wants to discuss the struggle within her marriage. She has four children and feels that if she were to have any more, she would not be able to care for them either financially or emotionally. She wants to look at some of the possible options available to her. You are a very warm, compassionate and understanding person. You listen carefully to her words and feelings, and give excellent responses. She feels understood and supported. As she mentions birth control, however, you (a very well-read and religious Catholic) begin to argue about this, your position being that this is not one of her options. She has felt your understanding and is now confused. You push a little harder, with quotes from Papal documents. She becomes defensive; you give her some loving and well-meaning words about her need to trust God. She begins to cry. Communication has broken down. No matter how you try to convince her, she is no longer able to talk to you about the situation. You have gotten caught up in overstanding.

SCENARIO:

A father and son are working together to make a family room out of a rough basement. The father has done odd jobs in construction, plumbing, and a little electrical work. The son is presently studying electronics and has been reading his dad's books on home repair. As they begin the job, the father tells the son how he wants to begin. They work well together for awhile; the father is about to explain a complicated electrical part of the job when the son challenges him. He just read something about it in Popular Mechanics and feels his father is wrong. The father has felt rather close to his son during this project and now feels hurt. The father defensively argues, reminding the son that he (the father) is in charge and proceeds to complete the task his own way. He has gotten caught up in the need for control.

Whenever we are in the role of *speaker/knower* we are really asking for a *listener*, one willing to understand us. When we have a truly understanding *listener*, we are able to share or work through some difficult situations. We feel connected in a very special way to the one who is understanding. If the *listener* stops understanding, the connection breaks. Either side may begin to 'overstand.'

The *speaker* may begin to stress even more strongly the original stand taken. Overstanding is a defense mechanism. When we feel attacked, we become hurt, confused. These are ways to defend ourselves, as does the woman in scenario one. Control and manipulation are also reactions of self-defense, as in the father's response in scenario two.

> *"We need to look at the...word 'stand.' This word suggests, first of all, the taking of a stand, or position, or a standing for a belief or value. ...[It] catches the overwhelming sense of self-investment, or total commitment and engagement..."*
> — *Understanding*
> Charles A. Curran

What about the *listener*? He or she may also begin to overstand. The *listener* also brings personal beliefs and values to this process and this is why I have asked you, as *listener*, to put them on the shelf...temporarily.

I am not asking you to deny your values. I am only asking you to put them aside when you are in the role of understander. When one tries to stand-for and to understand at the same time, neither one happens! You cannot be both *speaker* (one who stands for something) and *listener* (one who understands).

I have been part of a circle of six women who have been meeting together for almost ten years. We have walked through some pretty wild places in one another's lives. It has been a safe and supportive group for us because of two consistent parts of our bimonthly meetings:

1. A closing prayer which we call our Credo

2. Asking for the response we want during our sharing time.

Here is our Credo, our closing prayer:

"I am taking full responsibility to risk being real!

"To the greatest of our ability, we respond to our own needs and wants at every moment and trust that in doing so we will serve each other's greatest good.

"As I take increasing responsibility for myself, I become a more real, authentic, and credible person for you to interact with.

"If I give you feedback, I will take responsibility to tell you graciously about anything I experience that is in conflict with my needs or wants, trusting that we will enter into dialogue with open minds. Amen."

This Credo has the qualities that we need in both the listener and the speaker: a person who is able to be real, who is responsible for their own growth, and who is willing to receive and give information and listening responses that allow a connection between others.

The second consistent part of our meeting comes during our sharing process when each has time to tell of events since we last met. At this time we ask for the response we want from the group that night. These responses might be:

* I just want to tell my story

* I want the group to listen without offering solutions

* I want feedback. (By feedback we mean: what you think and/or feel about what I said and/or did.)

* I want advice or suggestions.

* I want to be challenged or confronted in some way.

The connection we ask for as a speaker is really a request for a supportive and encouraging listener for those tough places in our lives. These are requests we can ask of people who come with a desire to connect, to be honest, to share, hear, and speak the truth with love. Both listener and speaker must bring these qualities to any encounter if growth or healing is to take place. You, too, can handle those raw parts of your life if you have a partner or group who will practice listening with you and with whom you can take turns in the roles of speaker or listener.

As this process becomes more clear through practice, hopefully you will find that you can more easily put aside your own thoughts, values, beliefs, or ideas and stay on track with the speaker. When you need to verbalize your own beliefs, fears, hopes, or a need for decision-making, you may ask to be speaker and have another person who is aware of this method of listening be the one understanding you.

Remember, these are both *temporary* roles. They are not who you are; *they are what you do for one another.*

I know that in the large group presentations you are being asked to listen intensely for a long period of time. I truly am grateful for the gift of your understanding. I am able to share these insights only because you have put yourselves on the shelf during these presentations. The small group sessions allow each of you to be a *speaker*; to present your own 'stand' with the help of understanding *listeners*.

అఄౕ

A Re-Group

Whether you are reading this book by yourself or are part of a group of people taking a class, this is a good time to stop, stretch, practice listening, and re-group.

If you are reading the book as part of your efforts to improve yourself, stop and think for a moment. Is there a friend or family member who might be willing to let you practice listening to them? What you need from them would be their willingness to talk to you for 10 minutes about something that they are trying to figure out in their life, a problem they are having, or a situation they are trying to learn to navigate. Your task would be to practice your ability to listen and understand what they are going through without telling them what to do or judging them. Set a timer so you know when the 10 minutes is up, and thank them for allowing you to listen to them.

If you are leading a group taking the listening course, allow two volunteers to come to the center of the group. One will be the *speaker* and the other will be the *listener* for 10 minutes, and then they will reverse roles for another 10 minutes. Each will take a turn being *speaker* while the other practices responding as a *listener*.

Ask each *speaker* to choose a topic they are passionate about or are wrestling with, and to speak from the heart.

Use the Brief Encounter outline on pages 82-83 as a guide. When they are finished, ask them the following questions:

1. Would you comment on the 10 minutes from your perspective as a speaker (or listener) in a broad, general way?

2. Do either of you have any comments on any particular thing that was said, or anything about any personal mannerisms that may have aided or hindered your ability to speak?

3. What encouraged you to speak more freely? What stopped you?

4. Is there anything else that occurs to you about the ten minutes?

When finished with both volunteers, ask the larger group what they observed. Good questions to start this discussion might be: Was there anything that surprised you? Was there anything that impressed you?

Allow time for discussion among the volunteers and the group observers, as people will learn a great deal from one another during this discussion.

It is rare that you have the opportunity to not only hear such an interview, but to also have the chance to hear how the volunteers in the exercise say how they felt during it.

When I am teaching this course, I am always grateful for the two people who volunteer because it gives the whole group a chance to discover other nuances in the encounter and to have their assumptions or fears verified or corrected regarding how someone else is feeling.

࿇

DOODLE OR WRITE YOUR OWN PERSONAL THOUGHTS, NOTES, IDEAS, AND OBSERVATIONS HERE

Chapter 5

৵৹৻

CULTURAL INHERITANCE

As we continue to respond to and practice brief encounters with family, friends, neighbors, co-workers, or even strangers, we begin to realize that our beliefs and values come from sources beyond parents, peer groups, teachers, and significant others in our lives. Our community, church, and society, even our geographic location and ancestry form and shape the way we look at life. These influences are all part of a *cultural inheritance* that is created and shaped by a larger world than the one immediately surrounding us.

A look at the various threads that run through our history may help us understand not only why each of us may differ in many ways, but also why there are some basic assumptions we all share in common; assumptions that, because of general cultural acceptance, are part of a treasury of basic truths. As we look at these beliefs and assumptions in the context of history, we find that they are not so eternal as we may at first think.

POWER VS. COMMUNITY…OR POWER FOR COMMUNITY?

Power has acquired a bad name these days because it seems to signify 'power over' others. This dominating, controlling method of relating is often experienced in business and other institutions, including some religious organizations.

For the people who work within such structures, their attitudes toward power can – and often do – create an oppression that becomes slavery. Yet power can have another meaning. It can mean *power with* or *power for* someone or some organization.

When the person with intellectual gifts, economic goods, leadership skills, or other tools of power places these gifts at the service of the community, this gift becomes power *for* others, not power *over* others. Community is formed only when one is willing to share such gifts with one another. Perhaps a story will clarify.

Once upon a time there was a young boy who had wanted a baseball and bat for all of his life. He waited and waited, prayed and prayed. Finally, on his seventh birthday, his parents handed him a long narrow package. He knew it! The ball and bat! It didn't take him more than a minute to run out around the neighborhood and show off this great gift. One of the neighbor boys went up to him, took the ball, and said, "Great, let's play right now." The birthday boy grabbed his ball back saying, "Give me that back. It's mine." The neighbor boys walked away and left the young boy holding his birthday gift, a gift that could have created community, a sense of bonding, and shared fun, but he was unwilling or unable to share.

In many ways and in various circumstances, we are just like that birthday boy. We don't realize that we can't play ball, or music, or life, until all the instruments are available to everyone.

Question: How can we learn this truth not only at a physical level, but also at a deeper, spiritual level?

Answers:
* By letting go of the power we think we have over truth!
* By recognizing that there are many perceptions of the same event.
* By being willing to hear the inner truth of someone else with enough trust and the same respect we have for our own truths.

Let us look again at some of the qualities of a *listener*:
Non-judgmental
Non-defensive
Accepting
Understanding
These are not the words of *power over*! They are the words of a *listener* willing to establish an atmosphere in which the speaker may safely struggle with his or her own life situation no matter how messy or embarrassing. They are the qualities of one who is willing to walk compassionately with another and who, by their unconditional acceptance, also learns from the ideas, feelings, and beliefs of others.

THE SCIENTIFIC MODEL (DICHOTOMIZING)

One reason this generation approaches life from the view of *power over* while also holding the belief that there is one specific and correct answer to any given question comes from the scientific model. When early scientists found that it was possible to measure the distance, the rhythm, and sometimes even the size of the stars, it opened up enormous possibilities in other areas as well. Philosophers, artists, and psychologists, as well as scientists and mathematicians, began to apply the scientific methods of accuracy and predictability to everything, including the human person. The discovery of the mechanical movement of the heart and the parameters of one's blood pressure system suggested that humanity, like the earth, was predictable.

> *"It is not our purpose...to reject all the valuable implications that the word 'scientific' now has for us...In its basic meaning, 'scientific' suggests a free, unbiased, and genuinely open search for 'what is.' This can be called truth or reality as long as...we recognize we are always searching. ...This will not tie us down, then, to an excessively narrow meaning that always involves seeing people as problems... G.K. Chesterton's phrase, 'cutting heads to fit hats' catches this."*
>
> — *Understanding*
> Charles A Curran

In order to study and concretize this predictability, scientists, mathematicians, and philosophers split the human person, dividing us into body and spirit. The body then was studied separately from the human soul and psyche, and even the psyche of a person was analyzed with a view to measure and control our responses.

Great strides were made in medicine through the study of the mechanics of the body, its heart rhythms, blood pressure, pulse, and other internal systems. Tragically, however, the body began to be perceived as a machine that was almost unconnected with the emotions, feelings, and soul of a person.

Descartes, a gifted scientist and a brilliant mathematician of this early period introduced the strictly mechanistic idea of humanity. The psyche was seen by him as an entity that resided in the body, much as the astronauts of today are contained in the complicated machine that carries them into space. The human, according to Descartes, was his or her psyche dwelling within a machine-body most delicately designed to serve human needs, but still a separate entity. We are deeply influenced today by this idea of separation between body, psyche, and soul. Our inability to both express and hear the total person – feelings and emotions as well as ideas, facts, and thoughts – is an outcome of this Cartesian perception.

THE PSYCHOLOGICAL MODEL (CATEGORIZING)

Using the same type of measurable and observable research, psychologists also began to decide what was 'normal' and 'abnormal' behavior. They then carefully categorized this research, put the categories in huge text books, and checked out those who came for counseling by the way they fit into these categories. In themselves, the measurements were helpful. The weakness came when they became absolutes rather than signposts. Once again, a saying of Jesus might suggest where we are both in the area of medicine and in human psychology:

> "People were not made for the law,
> the law was made for people."
> *Mark 2: 27*

What began as a tool for understanding the human person eventually became a method of judgment in which there was little room for behavior that differed from the norm. In this method of treating the human person, 'experts' became the authority whose background and judgment also determined what was right and what was wrong with a person. The hope was to make the study of the human person as exact a science as astronomy! However, it also locked people into a bad/good, sick/well model of judgment more mechanical than human. The following story made me realize the damage this does to a person in the deepest part of their soul.

A new client came to see me a few years ago and with great fear and painful emotion, she shared the history of her past. I listened carefully to the events and the choices she had made at times when survival was her primary focus in life. The memory, hurt, and depression these past experiences still carried were raw and her final sentence was so significant! She asked, "Can you fix me?" The only answer that came as I put all the pieces together was, "No, because you aren't broken. You were born beautiful. You just have a lot of garbage inside that together, we will peel away." We did work together, and when she felt ready for closure, she thanked me especially for that sentence in our first session. She said she would never forget it, because for the first time in her life she felt hopeful and knew she would make it beyond the pain.

THE MATHEMATICAL MODEL

The world of mathematics was also part of this movement for exactness. The struggle within us to believe that there is one truth, one right answer, one correct way to do something comes from some of the mathematical insights that we have absorbed from our culture. In what we might call the 'mathematical model,' the basic premise is: "To be true and trusted, it must be mathematically analyzed and expressed in numbers until it is clear and correct."

Such a premise expects, even demands measurement, problem-solving, and of course the usual right/wrong, good/bad criteria by which one judges mathematics – but now used to judge people!

No wonder, when someone approaches us and asks us to listen, our first question is: "What's the problem?" This not only suggests that something is 'wrong,' but also that there is 'an answer.' And of course, we who are asked to listen are then expected to give the correct one.

In this search for the correct answer, we soon get involved in questioning and doubting as a way to sift the 'true' from the 'false.' The *listener's* questioning, in this mathematical sense, becomes more an attack than a way of supporting the *speaker*. Our use of questions comes from this history of what is called 'methodical doubt.' It is an effort to be exact. This exactness is helpful when one is measuring the length of a cupboard, but is it helpful, or even possible, when walking through life with a friend?

The word *quest* is a far better word for what we want to do here. A quest is a journey, a way of searching for a path that isn't quite clear. I am inviting you to 'quest' with me in this seminar. Questions, therefore, or doubt, or debate, do not belong in the relational system within which we wish to operate.

> *"Everything you possess of skill,*
> *and wealth, and handicraft,*
> *wasn't it first merely a thought*
> *and a quest?*
> — Jalaluddin Rumi

In the ways described above, (scientific, psychological, mathematical models) we were taught to relate to people in the same way that we relate to *things*! It is safer for us, more predictable. I am now inviting you to a new way of relating, one in which we are not objective bystanders with a slide-rule in hand, but rather I am asking you to be immersed in the mysteries of life. I also promise you it will be far from predictable!

Unlike the world of mathematics and science, human beings were never meant to be controlled. They were meant to learn, grow, and unfold the true spirit of the self. Because of the wonderful gift of free will and the unique differences in each of us, we will always be a surprise to ourselves and others. So what I am hoping you will do is experience this seminar as an adventure as we all plunge into the messiness of what it means to be human.

Key Moments in a New Paradigm

The above reflection on our culture and history hopefully shows us the legacies of our communication and why we approach one another the way we do. Our relationships have been structured on the model of mathematics; therefore, we scientifically mathematicize one another, categorize one another, and in the process, we depersonalize one another. Again, let me suggest that there are no villains. What we need is an awareness of these past inherited beliefs. Once aware, I hope you will be ever ready to ask: "What do we do now?"

Historically, we are already in the midst of a new way of seeing the world and each other. Even scientists and mathematicians recognize that this structure of absolute certitude doesn't always work in the arena of science and math, and especially not in the area of human beings.

The clearest breakthrough came in 1926 when a physicist named Heisenberg showed that the more we move into particle physics, the greater the resulting unpredictability. Now all we have to do is begin to apply this reality to our personal relationships!

Each of us is unpredictable. We don't know what we are capable of…nor do we always know how we might respond in a given situation. We do know that there are moments in our lives when we might be either at our best or at our worst. And it is during these key moments that we want or need a friend willing to be patient with us or excited with us.

This is the role of the *listener* who has learned to understand without control (power over), without categories (the psychological model), and without an expectation of perfection (the mathematical and scientific models). Therefore, by using what I will now call a *new paradigm*, the *speaker* can move out of a stuck position and continue their journey in peace.

This new paradigm recognizes that, although the age of science, which created our dichotomized, analytical world was somewhat helpful in many ways, it is not true that the human person is divided into two halves. Soul and body are not separate. They are deeply integrated and need to be honored as such.

The *listener*, by capturing both the cognitive (insights, ideas, thoughts) and the affective (feelings, emotions) aspects of the *speaker* will help him or her to once again become a whole person. It is this wholeness, found in the new paradigm that I will continue to stress as we move into the insights and ideas in the next chapter.

DOODLE OR WRITE YOUR OWN PERSONAL THOUGHTS,
NOTES, IDEAS, AND OBSERVATIONS HERE:

Course Outline of Day 3

᠙᠒

NON-DEFENSIVE LISTENING

Morning

Relational Dynamics: The Inseminational Model
  Metaphor of the Earth and Seed
  Trusting in outcomes beyond expectation
Scattered Communication
  Snags in the process
  Poor listeners
  Lack of Trust
  Hearing only the affective or the cognitive
  Confusion
Non-investment in the speaker or the information
The speaker's investment
Mixed Agenda of Speaker
  Preacher/Lecturer
  One who wants to Vent Feelings
  Victim
  Martyr
Practicing the Listening Process

Afternoon

Belief Systems That Affect Defensiveness
  Belief in *authority*
    The need for power or control
    The need to be 'right'
    Tradition and structure

Belief in *relationship*
    Personal involvement
    Values and Beliefs
    Creative change
Defensive Dynamics
    A Non-objective listener
    Personal involvement
    A need to be in control or be right
    Confusion of roles
Managing Various Responses
    Defensiveness and argument
    Venting and escape
    Death Wish
    Killing Oneself
    Killing Another
    Non-defensive Listening
Reconsidering All Communication Styles
    Discussing
    Questioning
    Debating
    Arguing
    Negotiating
    Convincing
    Listening
Advanced Listening/Reflection Process

Chapter 6

෨෧

Relational Dynamics: A New Model for Listening with Your Heart

A PARADIGM IS A SET OF EXPECTATIONS, ASSUMPTIONS, BELIEFS, and ideas of how the world works along with the habitual ways we respond to that world.

When we looked at some of the past paradigms that affect communication and relationships, we found images and attitudes based in science, mathematics, and psychology. As we investigate our new paradigm, let's use a new name and a new image of dynamic relationships, one that we will call the *Inseminational Model.*

The parable told by Jesus of the sower and the seed captures the dynamics of the *speaker/listener* model we have been studying.

> "A sower went out to sow his seed; and as he sowed, some fell along the path and was trodden underfoot or the birds of the air devoured it. Some fell on the rocks; and as it grew up, it withered away because it had no moisture. Some fell among the thorns; and

the thorns grew with it and choked it. And some fell
onto good soil and grew, and yielded a hundredfold."

Luke 8:5-18

In the *Inseminational Model,* the earth, the seed, and the
sower are absolutely vital to the process. Without any one of these
ingredients there would be no fruit, no harvest.

This image recognizes the value of both the earth and the
seed. So, in a sense, that is what is happening here. I, in some way,
have been scattering seed. You, like the earth, have been receiving
the seed in various ways. The more receptive and moist the earth,
the better the seed will expand and grow. Without the receptivity, it
might be somewhat like the rocks or the thorns – unable to give what
the seed needs to grow.

Notice here I am no longer talking about problems and
answers, but about seed and soil. The relationship between seed and
soil is not one of arrogance and superiority, but of interdependence
and cooperation. One without the other is useless.

It is possible that either the seed or the soil may be defective,
but that is not discovered until the seed actually enters the soil and
the two begin to work together. Any judgments about effectiveness
also cannot be immediately expected; it will take a certain amount
of time. A look at nature itself reminds us that the time taken for
harvesting depends on the seed...which is planted, as well as the
ground, in which it silently, invisibly grows.

Remember, this model is not based on prediction! A variety
of seeds can be found in human beings as well as in nature. Humans
grow within the womb in nine months; elephants take twenty-two
months. A bamboo tree doesn't become visible for six years after
its planting, and it takes eighty years for date fruit to appear. Every
seed has its own timetable for fruitfulness. I have been a teacher
and counselor for over thirty years. Many of the students have been

immediately grateful for what they have learned. However, there have also been letters of gratitude received five or ten years after the students have graduated. Was I more successful with the early bloomers or the late? Neither! Each seed has its own time.

> *"All children are gifted. Some just open their packages earlier."*
> — Michael Carr, Educator

Let us also reflect on the vulnerability of the sower. This story catches the notion of a person willing to place precious seeds into the ground with a confidence that they will not be wasted. The earth too, in its trust and willingness to open up to the seed, chooses to be equally vulnerable.

If we use this parable to describe the process of listening and speaking, we find a whole different way of relating to one another. The *listener* is like the ground – open and receptive to the words (seeds) of the *speaker*. The one who is speaking is like both sower and seed, wanting his or her ideas to be sensitively received. As we look at the process in this way, we might be able to understand why we have often been protective or hesitant to speak of anything but surface things. The willingness to take a chance on one another makes listening both difficult and precious.

Looking at this as an image for understanding and relating to one another, we can perhaps see that we are no longer in a structure of agreement-disagreement, or one of question-and-one-right-answer! There is no 'right' answer between us. There is, rather, the seed's and the soil's need to connect, to 'belong.' That is why all speakers struggle to become more clear as they share what they know. It is also why focused listeners continue to understand and reflect back what it is they hear at all levels.

A speaker/searcher may be asking if you really want to understand them. If I am the speaker and you are the listener, there is no way that you can physically check if you really do understand what I mean unless you give me, as speaker, a chance to say, "No, that isn't what I was trying to say," or, "Yes, that's what I meant."

For such a process to take place, we both must be invested in one another and in the understanding between us.

We, like the seed and the soil, want to become better and better at connecting. To carry Luke's image of seed and sower even further, the sower took the time and energy to prepare the ground and plant the seed because there was an ultimate trust that the harvest would come. In the same way, I trust that if we can begin to understand one another, something beyond both of us will come forth.

I truly believe that as I struggle to formulate words and feelings, there will come clarity and deeper insights that are greater than either of us alone. That is why questions-and-answers can be so limiting. They do not allow a third kind of possibility to be born. *I believe that this connection between us produces something beyond both of us*, and I want to be open to a surprise outcome that neither of us expected.

Therefore, it is important that neither of us come into communication with an already fixed agenda. We need to be true to values and beliefs that have proven to be true and helpful for our growth and peace, but we also need to hear one another's truth as we listen without power or ego.

The parable of the sower came from Jesus of Nazareth, whose own experience was true to the story. Many who heard him speak refused to listen. They came to him with a need for power. They had their own agenda, one they refused to change.

In this process of listening, the speaker/searcher is asking for a listening heart that is open to possibilities beyond the limits of the past. In the same way, I am not asking you to give up all that you value, I am only asking you to be open to other possibilities. I am suggesting that we move to communicating and relationships based on a new paradigm – that of the *Inseminational Model*. How will any of us stretch beyond ourselves unless we grow together?

SCATTERED COMMUNICATION

Let me now presume that we both truly want to begin acting out of this new paradigm that I have just described. We now recognize the limitations of the old paradigm and its historical models of problem-solving and question-and-answer.

We are perhaps even ready to plunge into a *relational* way of being with and *for* one another. Yet we find that our communication skills still run into snags. Surprise! To know something in our head does not necessarily mean we have it fully integrated into our soul. That is why our practice together here is so important. Hopefully, as we work together, I will be able, as the *knower* of this model, to show you areas where more practice is still needed. It will be like learning a second language, a second way of being, and is an excellent example of fine-tuning.

When immigrants first arrive in a new country, it is important for them to learn some basic words and phrases: food, transportation, money exchanges, and so on. They are initially clumsy but gradually their basic language skills improve. To refine these language skills, however, the learner must be willing to be corrected, to have a native speaker continue to polish the more elusive and challenging expressions. Often the insecure immigrant becomes confused, perhaps defensive. Communication often becomes scattered. The language teacher sometimes feels like giving up, but if this happens, the deeper learning stops. Our study of the Stages of Learning helps us understand some of the dynamics going on. If you recall, it is most likely in Stage 3 of the learning process that the problem of *ambiguity* comes up, which is when both the teacher and the learner want to be to be speaker, want to be understood. The result is scattered communication.

There are other reasons for scattered communication besides being at stage three in the learning process. The longer I teach this seminar, the more reasons I uncover for the closing down of communication.

I have a list of these reasons, and as you continue to learn and practice using your listening skills, you may uncover more ways that communication between two people hits a snag.

1. Poor or unskilled listener
2. Lack of trust within the speaker
3. Listener hearing only the affect (feelings, emotions)
4. Listener hearing only the cognitive (ideas, insights)
5. Confusion in the speaker or the listener
6. No investment by the listener in the speaker or the information
7. Inability on the part of the speaker to honor the process.

Poor Listeners

One of the advantages of learning in a live seminar is that everyone is focused on the process and the practice. The structure is one of disciplined listening, sometimes painful, but eventually helpful for developing both the skills and the qualities of a *listener*.

However, you can still learn a great deal by reading this book and finding someone to practice with.

When we are in a setting without the exterior structure created here, we may easily forget to hold to the position of *listener*. We sometimes quickly *stand-for or overstand* and forget to *understand*. We begin to argue, discuss, or change the subject. These communication dynamics aren't necessarily bad; they just aren't the role of one who understands. If there is confusion in communication it is often because we have not clearly remained in the position of one who listens…and *only listens*.

Earlier in this book I mentioned that when I attended my first listening seminar with Charles Curran, I was with a group of six at the same table for the duration of the week. We were all so committed to the method yet so aware of our need for more practice that we decided to meet once a month for a full day together.

> *"Many a man would rather you heard his story than granted his request."*
>
> —Phillip Stanhope
> Earl of Chesterfield

Our workshop was in November, and we met every month until the end of the school year in June. We were all very clear on the roles of speaker and listener. During each monthly meeting we had three sessions in which each of us took turns being speaker and listener for a period of ten minutes, using the format of the Brief Encounter.

The blessing of the decision to meet was that we came to know the process deeply and learned to make good contracts with each other. We also were honest when our listener was not true to the model and we held each other accountable for that role. This learning experience helped us to go beyond our own practice group to skillfully apply it to all of our encounters and relationships.

LACK OF TRUST

Most people come into relational situations with past experiences of pain. Family, work partners, or friends may not always have been trustworthy or supportive. No matter how much our head is ready to listen and apply the qualities of the listener's role, lots of 'buttons' may quickly be pushed!

As soon as we feel those inner defensive responses, we have a wonderful chance to be in touch with feelings coming perhaps more from the past than the present. These feelings often cause scattered communication on our part. It is also helpful to remember that the persons with whom we are talking bring their own past experiences and defense protections as well. Again, we need to remember that there are no villains...just be aware, monitor the feelings in yourself or others without judgment or blame.

HEARING ONLY THE AFFECTIVE OR ONLY THE COGNITIVE

Usually I have two facilitators assist with each listening seminar. In my seminars, I often ask the participants to choose a partner and take five minutes to be *speaker*, evaluate the experience, then switch roles with the other partner taking their turn to be *speaker*. While these two partners are sharing, the two facilitators also join in to observe and listen as partners in the process.

In one of my seminars, I invited two facilitators who had both helped me often, but neither of them had met the other. When the time period of partner-sharing was over, one of the facilitators asked to see me privately when I had a minute. At the first break, we disappeared together and she quietly asked me why I had chosen that particular other person as a facilitator. She felt her fellow facilitator had very poor skills in listening.

At the second break, the other facilitator came to me and reported the same experience of not having been heard by the first facilitator, a supposedly qualified listener. I knew both of them were good listeners and had worked effectively with small groups.

During the next large group interaction, I listened carefully to the responses that each of these facilitators had given and discovered an interesting fact. One of the facilitators consistently picked up the cognitive part of my presentation. She was excellent at understanding the ideas, insights, and philosophy I was sharing.

The other one caught mainly my feelings, emotions, and beliefs beautifully. Together, I was being heard, but each of them was missing a part of what was being expressed by the *speaker*! No wonder they didn't feel heard when they were partners!

As a *listener*, each facilitator was using the area she was most comfortable with rather than hearing the *speaker* at both levels – cognitive and affective. *Speakers* often move fluidly from their thinking to their feelings; sometimes they combine both. As *listeners*, our challenge is to follow the *speaker*. Is he or she sharing ideas and information, or is the stress on emotions or feelings?

Remember, we are working toward staying on track with the *speaker* regardless of what we, as *listeners*, do most easily. As we more skillfully establish an atmosphere of trust, *speakers* will begin to share their whole person – both feelings and ideas. It can block the *speaker* if the *listener* hears only one half of who they are!

> *"If we have no peace, it is because we have forgotten that we belong to each other."*
> — Mother Teresa

CONFUSION

Occasionally a speaker is so confused, fearful, or uncertain that the *listener* isn't able to follow the *speaker's* thoughts. It takes a great deal of skill and inner listening to help unravel some communications. If a *listener* has effectively developed both the technique and the caring qualities of listening, he or she will be able to pick up enough threads of the conversation to help the *speaker* become clear. But when one is just learning this listening process, the lack of skill on the part of the *listener* will further complicate the confusion. That isn't a reason to give up, however. Just know that it is part of the learning process. The confusion may come from the *speaker*, but it also may come from the *listener's* need for more practice. It has always been helpful to me to remember that, in my honest effort to understand, I am probably giving the *speaker* more support than he or she ever experienced before, no matter how clumsy I may be!

NO INVESTMENT BY THE LISTENER IN THE SPEAKER OR THE INFORMATION

A very important part of focused listening is investment. It is difficult enough to listen carefully when we care about the person or the subject matter. But when we are not invested, it is really a challenge! If you are freshly in love and the sun rises and sets on the person who is talking, listening can be fun. One needs little technique when your heart is involved. But if the *speaker* is not your favorite person and he or she is talking about underwater bird-calling, it may be impossible to stay focused for very long! Again, this doesn't mean one should quit. It only explains why *understanding* is more than a technique and also why the process may not always be smooth and clear.

THE SPEAKER'S INVESTMENT

When I choose to be a *listener* in this very disciplined way, I hope that my effort will help the *speaker* not only become more clear, but also discover new depths from within himself or herself. This doesn't happen effectively when there is not a strong desire in both the *speaker* and the *listener* to be connected in a relational and cooperative way. If the *speaker* wants the kind of agreement or debate that flows out of the mathematical, scientific model of relating, this method of listening doesn't work.

Let's look again at the earth/seed image. The new paradigm of the *Inseminational Model* of relating is especially appropriate here. If the seed doesn't want to grow in the ground, or doesn't want to trust and depend on the soil enough to be planted, obviously no fruit can grow. If the seed doesn't recognize its own personal role in the planting and growing process, it will not immerse itself in the soil. If the seed doesn't believe that only together with the earth does it have exactly what it needs to bring forth something new, how can it happen?

When we approach life in this kind of relational way, there are no absolute answers, but rather a desire to live one day at a time the best we can with the pieces we have at that moment. It is with this attitude, then, that *listening* becomes so helpful. It allows us to clear away the inner confusion so that we might better hear some creative options rather than absolute answers.

MIXED AGENDA OF THE SPEAKER

Speakers come in a variety of packages. As you practice listening, be alert to the qualities required by a *searching* speaker. When there is resistance or confusion, it may not be because you as listener are failing in some ways. The Brief Encounter described earlier isn't always possible, not because you aren't willing or able to listen, but because the various speakers you meet may have a mixed agenda. They may indeed want a listener, but they may not be a committed *speaker/searcher*. The three agendas I have met most frequently are:

1) Preacher/lecturer
2) One who wants to vent feelings
3) The victim or martyr

PREACHER/LECTURER – I have often been with people who want to be a preacher or lecturer rather than the kind of speaker who wants connection, understanding, and growth as a person. A preacher is one who thinks he or she is right; a lecturer is one who believes he or she knows what is true. They both believe there are absolute answers, and as the speaker they feel that they must defend them. These needs push the speaker to seek *agreement* from another rather than understanding. Again, if the speaker as preacher/lecturer wants the kind of agreement or debate that flows out of the mathematical, scientific mode of relating, this method of listening doesn't work. To clarify this statement a bit more, let us remind ourselves of the *qualities of a speaker* as found in the process we have been using throughout this book:

SPEAKER (client)

1. Knower
2. Searcher, clarifier
3. Needs and wants understanding
4. Desires to be heard
5. Desires to grow and change
6. Desires to be personally responsible
7. Desires to be open and trusting

One of the difficulties of a preacher/lecturer is that they often expect or require agreement. When this is the speaker's agenda, they become an expert, not a partner. They also presume that the listener's reflective response is an agreement rather than a mirror reflection of the speaker's own words and feelings. This presumption comes more from the authority model than the relational model of connection and support. You can certainly listen, yet there may not be any growth or movement in the speaker because that is not their personal agenda. Theirs is usually one of *convincing or debating.* You may learn some important information from them, but that is not *focused listening.*

The question in this listening model might be, "Do you want to be one of the people in a partnership...or the one who always needs to be in charge? My father had a great phrase about what we know and who we are: "What you know and do is only a hat you are wearing; it isn't who you *are.*"

ONE WHO WANTS TO VENT FEELINGS – Have you ever been part of a conversation where one of the participants sounds almost like they are on a speeding train that carries them and their feelings forward at full speed? Some speakers are so obsessed with either themselves, past pain, or present passions and emotions that they are unable to clarify, let go, and move on. The image of a mirror is so helpful here. Why do we look into a mirror if not to check something that may need to be fixed, adjusted, or changed? We as listeners offer to be that mirror, but the person isn't able to hear or recognize this because they are stuck somewhere in their life. It could be a place of success and they cling to it for its value...it may be past suffering that needs healing, but seems to give them some virtue.

I have had clients that tell the same story over and over, and the more they tell it, the deeper they are stuck. I have a phrase for listeners that has been powerful with this kind of speaker, "Don't fix it, don't fight it, don't feed it, just name it."

When I hear a story of pain, I hear not just the words but also their need to hang onto the pain, somewhat like a martyr. I say "That is the third time you have shared that. Do you want to do anything about it?"

As listener, it isn't yours to fix. We are not the source of grace or power. We can walk through it with them, but if a speaker wants to vent rather than seek change, even a listening heart isn't enough. One can only love them, accept their choice, and move on.

There may be times in our lives when, even with skilled listening the speaker chooses not to grow or change. We must let them go; let them do what they have to do. There are ways to be present to those we love without becoming part of their pattern.

VICTIM – Is isn't hard to recognize a victim when you begin to listen with both your head and your heart. There are people unable to accept and work with their own limits, mistakes, or failures. Victims are often people who feel helpless in the midst of what life itself brings. When difficult things happen they often seek for cause or blame outside themselves. When they are listened to with compassion, they say and feel, "It's my parents' fault...my background...my neighbors... my teachers...or even God's fault. If only they had or had not...(put in any person or situation)...I wouldn't be in this shape." The stories are endless. Some seek solace from others, not for growth but for sympathy or agreement. Some almost brag about how awful life or people have been.

There are many reasons for this behavior. Each person has their own reasons. When I listen and name the truth of their position of 'victimhood,' I always ask *why* a person is choosing to remain in that situation because I truly don't know why. It is important to ask that question, not only for the person's sake but also for our sake as a compassionate, understanding listener. When one listens with the heart, we often find that they really aren't choosing it. They may not even know they are a victim. They also may not have the slightest idea how to get out of it. And often, because they are so alone, they can't get out of particular situations. This is where our presence as a focused listener is such a gift. When we know we are not alone, it is amazing how we are able to look at other possible options even in the most horrendous of circumstances.

It is also in such non-judgmental questioning that we discover the people who are victims by choice. Some become defensive and give reasons why they remain in that position. Others truly ask themselves "why" and find a path out of the feeling of helplessness. They still may suffer because life isn't fair. But naming what you, as a listener pick up, offers the truth spoken in love that they may embrace.

MARTYR – Victims and martyrs show some of the same behaviors, but their motives are different. Martyrs are coming from a place in themselves that seeks to view the struggle, pain, and suffering in their lives as a spiritual dynamic, maybe even a special mission given to them by God. In the history of some religions, martyrdom is like a red badge of courage. Even so, it still comes from the feeling of helplessness, but martyrs believe it shows virtue rather than powerlessness. If we ourselves are martyrs, or we meet them in our focused listening experiences, we might ask the following questions;

* Is this suffering from ego or from Spirit?
* Is this something I am creating and maintaining, or is it what life brings to me?
* Is it something I need to change through healthier choices and prayer, or to accept?

How do we remain faithful beyond any agenda?

We, too, could be any of these speakers with an agenda of our own. However, if we approach life in a relational, connected way such as in the metaphor of the seed and the earth, there are no absolute answers we seek, but rather a desire to live the mystery of life one day at a time the best way we can with the pieces we have at the moment. It is with this attitude then, that listening becomes so helpful. It allows us to clear away the inner confusion so that we might better hear some creative options rather than the security of absolute answers. St. John of the Cross caught well the mystery of such trust when he said:

> "If a person wishes to be sure of the road he trods on, he must close his eyes and walk in the dark."

WHEN PRACTICING THE LISTENING PROCESS

Keep these points in mind:
1. The need to be heard beyond the words (pg. 120)
2. The Stages of Learning (pgs. 87-89)
3. Personal stance in the process (pgs. 92-95)
4. The Brief Encounter (pgs.78-80)
5. Cultural inheritance (pg. 101)
6. Dynamics of *relationship* vs. *laws and rules* (pgs. 61-63)

Then:
1. Choose someone in your life who is willing to practice with you these skills of both listening and speaking. Together, read the entire story of the Sowing of Seed from Mark 4:1-20.

2. Reflect and discuss this story in the following way: One of you becomes the listener who will do the reflecting, and one becomes the speaker for five minutes while sharing responses to the following questions:
   a) What did you understand and hear the author to be saying when you read this story?
   b) How did you feel about the story?
   c) What values, beliefs, and experiences did you recall from your own life as you read the information in the story?
   d) How will this story change your communication or deepen what you think or do in the future?

3. When the five minutes is up, the speaker takes another five minutes to let the listener know how well he felt heard and understood. Use the Brief Encounter form on page 82-83 as a suggested way to share your experience as a speaker. Then Switch

Roles and repeat the above process. Use this process for any area of life where you would like a skilled listener to help you understand, clarify, and grow.

REFLECTION PROCESS AFTER THE BRIEF ENCOUNTER

1. Was there scattered communication?

2. Were there mixed agendas of the speaker?

3. Were there beliefs that create defensiveness?

4. Were there defensive dynamics?

5. What were other possible responses by the listener?

6. Would it be helpful to reconsider all communication styles?

DOODLE OR WRITE YOUR OWN PERSONAL THOUGHTS, NOTES, IDEAS, AND OBSERVATIONS HERE:

Chapter 7

ॐ⊷

BELIEF SYSTEMS THAT CREATE DEFENSIVENESS

IN OUR FIRST SESSION WE LOOKED AT THE MODEL OF LEARNING that operates when one bases life on laws and rules alone. In that model, the stress is on authority, judgment, absolute truths, and right or wrong. Much of that belief system stems from the historical influence of the predictable and controllable discoveries of science and mathematics. Out of that perspective came a way of relating to one another that was more mechanical than relational. Human beings were expected to run like machines and when we didn't, when we were not predictable, we were often judged as wrong or 'irrational' (notice the mathematical terminology). This way of seeing the world and the human race led us to a way of relating that is far from relational. Because rules, laws, and authority were the primary values in this system, our way of responding to one another was consistent with it.

Let us review the Authority Model of life based on *Authority, Laws,* and *Rules:*

1. We need to be 'right'
2. We need power and control
3. Our structures, habits, and traditions are valued more than individuals or creative change

It is from this authority model that much of our defensiveness comes. When we believe that there are 'absolute truths' in personal relationships and that one can discover and prove these absolutes (as in science), then we will pursue such truths. We will attempt to find and enforce rules as absolutes. We will want to be correct. We will follow those who present an illusion of absoluteness and security. When we do this, truth is sought outside of ourselves in afar-off, hierarchical authority.

If I feel I have discovered this 'absolute truth,' I will seek power and control in order to impose that 'truth' on others. Eventually, structures, habits, and traditions will be built to protect these 'truths.' We begin to lose the spirit of 'questing' and we question, challenge, and debate anyone who does not fall in line with the structures we have built. Of course, we will argue if we feel there is only one right way to know or act or be. As we have already pointed out, who wants to be wrong?

However, if we can nurture the belief that every person has a piece of the truth, and that each perspective of an event was accurate for the person doing the perceiving, there would be no need to prove that we are right!

How often have we said: "Your perspective depends on your point of view," or perhaps, "It depends on which side of the fence you're on." These are excellent idioms that describe the new paradigm of relating – not as machines, but as unpredictable, questing, learning people.

When life is seen as relational rather than mechanical, there is less need to be in control. Values and beliefs are shared and shaped by a community rather than any one authority figure who must hang on to power at whatever price. And as life becomes communal, there is less need to be 'right.' Defensiveness is no longer a strong response to others when we know that there are many ways to cut carrots!

In the past few years my family has experienced the deaths of my father and all of his brothers and sisters. We are from a tradition of storytelling people and now my father's family storytellers are all gone. I don't want to lose that tradition in my mother's family, so I have been carrying a tape recorder with me whenever I go to her home for the family feasts and celebrations. We are now taping such wonderful tales and each story has its own flavor.

It was tricky at first not to argue about what 'really happened.' Now I just want to hear how the rest of the family experienced what I used to think only I knew! Often we tell the same story many times in order to add to the collection for the latest nieces and nephews. Even as we re-tell the story, there are additions! Why? Because life really ISN'T just rules and laws! It is about love and relationships. Tradition isn't something you write in stone; it is something alive, changing, and stretching like a healthy plant growing new leaves.

What does all this have to do with listening? When I am listening to another person, several things are happening inside of me. One thing involves my own beliefs and perceptions. In spite of what I know about relational ways of listening, often some very deep beliefs get challenged.

When I find myself becoming defensive, it automatically sets off an alarm. I know immediately something important is happening that I need to pay attention to because doing so brings me a little more insight into myself. I know myself better, which leads eventually to being able to understand others better. The book, *A Course In Miracles*, has a great quote for this inner knowing:

"Truth Needs No Defense"

If I feel sure about something for myself, I find little need to fight about it! And when I remember that everyone's perception depends on what side of the fence they are standing on, I have less need to argue. It might be wiser just to go walk on their side of the fence through the use of a listening heart.

In a world of machines, judgments of right or wrong, and irrational people, we fear for our emotional and intellectual safety. Defensiveness is a protection against such fear. However, as we become more convinced that we are not machines and we don't HAVE to be right all the time, it will become easier to put ourselves temporarily on the shelf and hear the wisdom and experience of others.

As the image of the seed and soil become a way not only of thinking but of *living*, we will want to be open, receptive, and trusting. Harvests only grow when the sower risks planting a seed and the ground is willing to embrace it. Attacking the seedling because you do not think it is growing correctly only results in an empty harvest.

> *"It is not the absence of defensiveness that characterizes learning, but the way defensiveness is faced."*
> — Peter Senge

Defensive Dynamics

A Non-Objective Listener

Defensiveness is a protective response in human communication. Not all of it comes from belief systems based on the idea of authority, rules, and control. We know that defensiveness depends not only on *what* was said but on *who* said it! There are times when both the information and the *speaker* trigger a strong emotional response.

Yet what else is going on when we, as *listeners*, are not objective? Perhaps that has already happened during this seminar, both in a negative and in a positive way. There may have been things you heard during my presentations that made you want to scream: "Stop! That isn't my experience!" There may have been other things that made you want to cheer.

This lack of objectivity is not necessarily either bad or good. *It only indicates that someone or something is important to us.* It also shows that we are very much involved either emotionally or intellectually in what is being said. It certainly helps me when you are invested and involved in what I am sharing with you! It is important that you stay cool and clear, but still engaged. Indifference is not the best way to listen. *Awareness* is really the goal. When we become aware of defensiveness, the feeling can invite us to discover something new...or create resistance.

Personal Involvement

The kind of emotional or intellectual involvement mentioned above can become very intense when we are deeply affected by what we hear. I can clearly recall a time when those of us in my family did hear and experience just such a painful reaction.

My family lived in Pontiac and my father worked for the Michigan Employment Security office at this time. Every three years he took a civil service test and always scored among the top three on the tests. In 1941, he was promoted to Detroit and we moved to a suburb called Ferndale. We all attended St. James Parish School and loved it! We were very happy there.

In 1950, he took another test and was promoted to Saginaw, a city across the state. At the time, there were six of us in the family – my parents and four girls. My oldest sister was preparing for marriage and would not be involved in the outcome. I had already moved to Nazareth as a Sister of St. Joseph. My youngest sister was two years old and had no history of connection to St. James School. However, my sister, Corrine, was in her last year of high school. It was my mother and Corrine who were most deeply affected when the news was shared about the coming move. Corrine simply refused to move. My mother, usually a supportive listener to my father, was also resistant. She, like Corrine, would have her entire world turned upside down. Of course their reaction was strong! We were all affected, but not with the deep emotional reaction that comes when one's whole life is about to be radically changed.

In this situation, my father became the *listener*. He accepted the position in Saginaw, but he allowed my mother and sister to live in Ferndale until Corrine finished the school year. Only then did they move to join him.

How can one be objective in such a personal situation? Because we are relational people, objectivity is not always possible. In such a personal situation it is normal to react. Resistance is not bad or good, it just is. Yet if we stay in that reactive mode, which many do, we break the connection that is required for personal and family or community growth.

It is at times like this that everyone needs to take turns being speaker and listener! Everyone's feelings need to be heard. Decisions must be made, but with less autocracy and more understanding so that many options may be investigated. My father's ability to do that made it possible to keep the family connection intact and to heal from the reactive resistance.

A Need to be in Control or a Need to be Right

One way in which I sometimes trigger defensiveness in others is when I think I know something VERY important and I want everyone to know it, even if they never asked! When that happens, it is coming from my desire to be the *knower* (speaker) rather than the *learner* (listener). This, too, is a subtle need to be in control or to be the 'wise one' with all the right information.

I am becoming better and better at recognizing when the person or people I am with become resistant. They, too, may know some of what I sometimes arrogantly declare. What they know may be in direct contradiction to what I am saying, with a kind of authority, to those I assume to be *listeners* (which they didn't agree to be in the first place)! The result – they also become *speakers*. Whenever there are two *knowers* there will be no *listeners* or *learners*! Both are asking to be understood, to be heard, to be supported. And when understanding isn't given, or when the insights differ, both often become defensive.

Confusion of Roles

In the example given above, you may have noticed that most of the time when resistance or defensiveness happens, people switch roles. No matter how skillfully you or I might begin as *listener*, when conflict starts we all want to be understood. Most of the time, the emotions are too intense to be able to even recognize that this is what is happening. In the next chapter, we will look at some of the many ways we respond to these defensive dynamics.

DOODLE OR WRITE YOUR OWN PERSONAL THOUGHTS, NOTES, IDEAS, AND OBSERVATIONS HERE:

Chapter 8

ॐॐ

MANAGING VARIOUS RESPONSES

In Closing

AS WE BECOME MORE AWARE OF THE DYNAMICS THAT CREATE defensiveness, we also become more able to respond creatively and freely to those dynamics. The word *respond* is key here. We often *react* instead of respond.

Defensiveness and argument are usually a reaction. Argument may be a response if our belief system comes from the Authority Model described earlier. If we believe that there is only one right answer, we will argue either until the other person is convinced... or we change our belief to match theirs... or the relationship ends!

If we believe that there is more than one side to a fence, or that there are lots of ways to cut carrots, defensiveness and arguments become less necessary.

Venting and Escape

As we have already said on page 125, the word *venting* describes the constant, almost obsessive talking that one does when he or she is upset, uncomfortable, or unaware. This may be a defense mechanism coming out of fear. Often it can be helped by a caring, understanding *listener*. Sometimes, however, good listening cannot help. There have been times when such 'talkers' go around and around as if on a wheel and even the most practiced listener isn't helpful. The venting just won't stop. This may be a situation when a professional counselor may be needed.

The art of listening, as I mentioned earlier, is only one of many tools used by professional counselors and therapists. In this case, the person may need more tools than the simple, albeit powerful, listening we have been practicing. This is true also of the person who might continually avoid the kind of deep listening/speaking commitment we have made in this seminar.

Notice that I use the word *continually* in the sentence above. I use this distinction as a contrast to the times when, personally, I just don't want to be either a *speaker* or a *listener*. Sometimes I just want to chat, or go on about underwater birdcalling…the small talk that takes no energy or thought. But when one *continually* avoids sharing feelings, hopes, dreams, or ideas with others, even those most closely connected with them, he or she needs more than a *listener* for relational connections to be restored.

We are not, however, responsible for *making* a person share deeply. Human communication is a choice freely made. I am grateful to each of you for having made that choice during these sessions.

It is because of this respect for freedom that I asked you, in our first session together, to make a contract with me. Under that common contract, I then described the qualities I would ask of you, the *listener*, and I promised to stay within my role as *speaker*.

DEATH WISH

Charles Curran, the originator of the *Listening Course*, talked about refusing to become a whole person as a way of dying. There are many ways of dying. Sometimes I describe listening as a sort of *dying to oneself*. I use this symbolic dying in a positive way.

Again, the image of Jesus of Nazareth comes to me with this phrase. He is often described as one who died to himself. He also asked his disciples to be like a seed, willing to fall to the ground and die in order to bring forth

> *"The unwillingness of a person to take on too much 'being' signals a kind of death-instinct, since to stay in non-being is seemingly one's final end."*
> — *Understanding Charles A Curran*

fruit. As we have already mentioned, the invitation he made was, "Die to yourself that others might live." *(John 12:24)*

These images of death are a way of catching what is happening in the interaction between a *listener* and a *speaker*. You have been putting your own ideas, feelings, and beliefs on the shelf in order to hear the ideas and beliefs I am presenting. "Putting yourself on the shelf" is a kind of dying to oneself. It is a temporary act of giving something up so that another might be free to speak. In this sense, dying is a positive act. There are two other kinds of death, however, that are not positive. Let us examine each of these.

KILLING ONESELF

Dying to one's self is a gift. It includes the ability to resurrect the self and to harvest new life. Killing one's self is suicide and there are several ways to do this. One can literally take their own life, but there is another kind of death that happens when we bury our feelings rather than put them temporarily on the self. It is the kind of suppression that pretends we do not have feelings. It denies our desire to be deeply heard by another. It is the deadening of our own insights and ideas. It is allowing others to dominate and silence us. To allow others to listen to us will avoid that kind of suicide.

To 'die to oneself' in order to listen compassionately to another is *not* suicide. It is simply putting your own thoughts and feelings aside for a short time. Then too, we must also have our turn to be heard. That is why I refer to *listening* and *speaking* as *roles*. We aren't play-acting, however. Rather, we are taking on each role for a while so that we, or another might have a chance to live.

KILLING ANOTHER

The absence of listening leads to another kind of death. I call it *killing another*. It isn't physical murder, but it does affect a part of us that sometimes feels destroyed. Sarcasm, insults, refusal to hear the feelings, dreams, and insights of another is deadening! Often our own resistance to sharing the deepest part of ourselves comes from the experience of having once felt this kind of death.

As a child, I used to sing: "Sticks and stones may break my bones, but names will never hurt me." When we have trusted another, and then feel betrayed, this may be a difficult song to sing.

What I want to get across here is how deeply we are affected when we have no one to listen to us in an accepting way. This way of hearing others in their weakness and struggles as well as in their strength and joys will help them avoid this kind of 'death.' To listen is to give life, not take it. And to feel heard is truly a life-giving experience to be treasured.

NON-DEFENSIVE LISTENING

I wanted to discuss the images of death described above before I invited you to use the art of listening in a totally non-defensive way that can be really tricky. This occurs when you are verbally attacked. When you have been attacked, your first reaction is to defend. That is where the idea of defensiveness comes from. You feel someone has walked into your space and said something that hurt or faulted you. The result is that you feel attacked.

A few years ago a frequently heard quote was, "Don't get mad; get even." I am introducing another possible quote, "Don't get mad; listen." Getting even just keeps going and going and the hurt never stops. But sometime, somewhere, someone has to stop. Listening changes the energy from defensiveness to understanding. It isn't easy, but it does have a powerful effect. Sometimes we may not do it. Perhaps on some days we might not even *want* to listen. But it is one option. Now you know how to do it, so you have one more choice.

RECONSIDERING ALL COMMUNICATION STYLES

At the beginning of my seminars I draw a circle and inside it write some skills that are often the focus in other communication workshops. These skills include:

1. Discussing
2. Questioning
3. Debating
4. Arguing
5. Negotiating
6. Convincing
7. Listening

Each of these are ways to communicate verbally with one another. Some of them are so frequently used we don't need a whole lot of practice. Most of them are carefully considered communication skills.

When I listed them in our first session, I commented on the value they might have in any human communication setting. However, at that time I also stressed that I would only concentrate on *listening*. The others may be useful, but I explained that I would not teach them in this seminar.

During the past few days we have indeed concentrated on listening. I have described some of the basic issues involved in listening and we have practiced the art of listening together. In both small and large groups, you have put your own ideas aside, temporarily, in order to intensely and sensitively listen to me and to one another. Hopefully, you have also been heard in the same way.

Now that we have considered various aspects of communication in human relationships, looked at what is involved in the skill of listening, and even practiced it, it might be a good time to return to these other skills.

As I have already made clear, I will not be teaching any one of them specifically. I just want to suggest that if we put *listening* at the top of this list, we will better know which of the rest we might most effectively choose when communicating with others in any setting. I will now look at these various skills in the light of *listening* itself, and the role listening plays with each of them.

Discussing

When people 'discuss,' it usually concerns a common topic to which those who are involved address themselves. Depending on how important the topic is to the participants, the time and intensity can be long and strong. Discussion stresses the 'speaking' element of communication and everyone adds their own opinions, information, experiences, and insights.

If we add *listening* to this particular skill (discussing), the noise level often goes down, the intensity is less, and clarification takes place more quickly. This allows the discussion to flow creatively rather than become argumentative.

QUESTIONING

The most common way of learning today is through questioning. I describe questioning here as 'a means to gain information, data, directions, and facts.' This definition presumes that there is an answer that is able to be communicated factually. Questions are more likely to involve the cognitive level of human exchange than the affective – or feeling – level.

The word *question* in its common usage seldom means *questing*, which means 'to seek.' Often, 'to question' means 'to challenge.' Therefore, when one is questioning another, instead of *questing*, one is often either challenging or listening for a specific piece of information. Seldom are they *listening* in order to understand the whole person who is speaking.

DEBATING

Webster's dictionary defines debate as: "controversy, argument; to discuss, to argue in detail, to reflect." Any listening that takes place in a debate situation usually has rebuttal for its purpose rather than understanding. Within the professional debate, there is usually a winner and a loser. While debating is never a benefit to *listening*, listening is always a benefit to debating!

ARGUING

Do we need any practice in the skill of arguing? How quickly I find myself doing this quite well! Arguing usually happens when two people feel very strongly about the same thing. They usually believe there is a correct answer or piece of information (like how to get from Detroit to California).

If the answer is indeed factual, there may be a way to find it. My suggestion is to listen to what each of you is saying and see what you know in common. I believe it is in the area of arguing that the art of *listening* is most vital and most likely to lead to a resolution that both parties can live with.

NEGOTIATING

Listening is absolutely essential in the arena of negotiation! When one is negotiating, it is usually for the purpose of coming to some acceptable ground for agreement. Negotiation is most possible when it begins with the kind of *listening* that leads to clarification. In this situation, I suggest that both parties begin with a specific time for *listening* and clarifying. When both feel heard and understood, real and positive negotiation can then take place.

CONVINCING

When one hopes to convince a person of something, it is helpful to find out their needs, expectations, hopes, dreams, and belief systems. You may find that they don't really need to be convinced because they already agree! On the other hand, you may find that some people have no intention of being convinced because you and they are worlds apart in beliefs and hopes. This information can best be discovered by *listening* and reflecting back what you hear. You will also find some who 'waver' quite a bit. Slick sales programs are designed to either break down the resisters or convince the doubtful.

LISTENING

By now you know that the kind of *listening* I am talking about in this course does not make slick listening a priority. I do hope that from your own experience of having been heard and understood, you can see, feel, and know the value of *listening* to another without any need for personal control.

To bring all of this together, we can say that ordinary communication makes use of words in various ways designed to inform and influence. *The Gift of a Listening Heart* is a model that combines words with a deep listening experience in order to create a deeper kind of communication. It is designed to help clarify, transform, and bring life to our own lives and the lives and hearts of those with whom we live and work.

Thank you for reading this book and/or coming to the seminar to learn. Let us hope that by listening to one another, we can make our world a better place to live.

అంశం

> *"The most basic of all human needs is the need to understand and be understood The best way to understand people is to listen to them."*
> —Ralph Nichols

PRACTICING ADVANCED LISTENING/ REFLECTION PROCESS

Keep these points in mind and watch for...
1. Scattered communication (pg. 117)
2. Mixed agendas of the speaker (pg. 123)
3. Beliefs that create defensiveness (pg. 133-134)
4. Defensive dynamics (p. 137)
5. Possible responses you can make as a listener (pg. 143)
6. Reconsidering all communication styles (pg. 147)

Then:
1. Begin to recognize when others seem to want a 'listener.' Use the Brief Encounter Form for Listeners outlined above (pgs.82-83) to gauge the situation you are in.
   * Contract part A:
      * Listen to a speaker for a couple of minutes and give a brief listening response.
      * If the speaker continues to share after you have given a listening response, continue to listen and respond.
      * If they do not, let it go and move to a dialogue.

2. If the speaker continues to be comfortable with you as focused listener, you can presume they have accepted the role as speaker and you can move to the more advanced applications of this process:
   * Contract part B
      * Most people are very grateful to be a speaker and perhaps even amazed that someone would listen with interest and respect. When this happens, it gives you a great opportunity to practice listening skills. As you practice more and more, you will find that you will be able to recognize more quickly

each speaker's purpose for staying connected to the process with you.

3. As your skill increases, you can then move to the next two parts of the Brief Encounter contract:

    * Contract part C
        * Monitor your own dynamics during the process
    * Contract part D
        * Recognize when the speaker has moved beyond the issue the two of you originally shared.

DOODLE OR WRITE YOUR OWN PERSONAL THOUGHTS, NOTES, IDEAS, AND OBSERVATIONS HERE:

Full Course Outline

Day 1
A Non-Abrasive Way to Relate

Morning

Different styles of communication

Difference between focused listening and ordinary communication

The difference between listening and giving advice

Roles of Speaker and Listener

Qualities of Listener (learner)
- Suspends judgment
- Caring & understanding heart
- Respectful
- Non-defensive
- Accepting
- Trustworthy
- Confidential

Qualities of Speaker (knower)
- A Knower, "giving birth to self"
- Searching, clarifying
- Needs understanding
- Desires to be heard
- Desires to grow & change
- Wants to be responsible
- Wants to trust

Structure Used in the Art of Listening

Afternoon

Belief systems as barriers
- Seeing life as 'laws and rules'
  - Authority
  - Right or wrong
  - Judgment

Seeing life as 'relationships'
  Understanding
  Support
  Acceptance and trust
Unconscious and Non-Verbal dynamics involved
    Belief systems
    Unconscious blocks
    Attitudes toward power and community
    Past experiences
Physical and Psychological need to hear one's own words and feelings
    Helps clarify confusion within oneself
    Shows acceptance and care from the listener

Day 2

BELONGING AND THE STAGES OF LEARNING

Morning

Brief Encounter and Focused Listening
  Affective content
  Cognitive content
  Values and Beliefs

Brief Encounter Form

Stages of Learning
  Stage 1 - Dependency
  Stage 2 - Opening to Learning
  Stage 3 - Navigating Ambiguity
  Stage 4 - Fine-tuning and Understanding
  Stage 5 - Interdependence

Personal Stance in the Communication Process
  Standing for
  Understanding
  Overstanding

Confusion
Defensiveness
Control
Manipulation
ReGroup

Afternoon

Cultural Inheritance
    Power vs. community
 Scientific model
       Dichotomized person
Psychological model
      Categories
Mathematical model
      Analysis
      Problem-solving
      Role of questioning or doubt
New paradigm: key moments

Day 3
NON-DEFENSIVE LISTENING

Morning

Relational Dynamics: The Inseminational Model
    Metaphor of the Earth and Seed
    Trusting in outcomes beyond expectation
Scattered Communication
    Snags in the process
    Poor listeners
    Lack of Trust
    Hearing only the affective or cognitive
    Confusion

Non-investment in the speaker or the information

The speaker's investment

Mixed Agenda of speaker
    Preacher/Lecturer
    One Who Wants to Vent Feelings
    Victim
    Martyr
Practicing the Listening Process

Afternoon

Belief Systems That Create Defensiveness
    Belief in *authority*
        The need for power or control
        The need to be 'right'
        Tradition and structure
    Belief in *relationship*
        Personal involvement
        Values and Beliefs
        Creative change
Defensive Dynamics
    A Non-objective listener
    Personal involvement
    A need to be in control or be right
    Confusion of roles
Managing Various Responses
    Defensiveness and argument
    Venting and escape
    Death Wish
    Killing Oneself
    Killing Another
    Non-defensive Listening
Reconsidering All Communication Styles
    Discussing
    Questioning

Debating
Arguing
Negotiating
Convincing
Listening

Advanced Listening/Reflection Process

BIBLIOGRAPHY

❧❧

Colt, Lee, *Listening: How to Increase Awareness of Your Inner Guide*; Swan Publishing Co., 1985.

Curran, Charles A., *The Cognitive Client: A Counseling-Learning Model*; Apple River Press, 1982.

Curran, Charles A., *Counseling and Psychotherapy: The Pursuit of Values*; Apple River Press, 1978.

Curran, Charles A., *Understanding: An Essential Ingredient in Human Belonging*; Apple River Press, 1978.

Curran, Charles A., *Counseling-Learning in Second Languages*; Apple River Press, 1976.

Curran, Charles A., *Counseling-Learning: A Whole Person Model for Education*; Grune & Stratton, 1972.

Curran, Charles A., *Psychological Dynamics in Religious Living*; Herder and Herder, 1971.

Curran, Charles A., *Religious Values in Counseling and Psychotherapy*; Sheed and Ward, 1969.

Green, Bernard D., *Counseling, Values and Learning*; Counseling Learning Institute, 1986.

Green, Bernard D., *Counseling and Advice-Giving in Pastoral Care*; Apple River Press, 1987.

Hart, Thomas N., *The Art of Christian Living*; Paulist Press, 1980.

Koile, Earl, *Listening as a Way of Becoming*; Regency Books, 1977.

Rardin, Jennybelle and Tranel, Daniel D., *Education in a New Dimension*; Apple River Press, 1988.

Sanford, John A., *Between People*; Paulist Press, 1982.

Tannen PhD., Deborah, *You Just Don't Understand Me*; William Morrow & Co. Inc., 1990.

CPSIA information can be obtained
at www.ICGtesting.com
Printed in the USA
FSOW01n1843230717
36475FS